Career Launcher

Law Enforcement and Public Safety

Career Launcher series

Career Launcher

Law Enforcement and Public Safety

Amy Hackney Blackwell

Ferguson Publishing
An imprint of Infobase Publishing

Career Launcher: **Law Enforcement and Public Safety**

Ferguson
An imprint of Infobase Publishing
132 West 31st Street
New York NY 10001

Library of Congress Cataloging-in-Publication Data

Hackney Blackwell, Amy
    Law enforcement and public safety / Amy Hackney Blackwell. — 1st ed.
       p. cm. — (Career launcher)
    Includes bibliographical references and index.
    ISBN-13: 978-0-8160-7956-8 (hardcover : alk. paper)
    ISBN-10: 0-8160-7956-0 (hardcover : alk. paper)
1. Law enforcement—Juvenile literature.
2. Public safety—Juvenile literature. I. Title.
    HV7922.H27 2010
    363.2—dc22

                                            2010044117

Ferguson books are available at special discounts when purchased in bulk quantities for businesses, associations, institutions, or sales promotions. Please call our Special Sales Department in New York at (212) 967-8800 or (800) 322-8755.

You can find Ferguson on the World Wide Web at http://www.fergpubco.com

Produced by Print Matters, Inc.
Text design by A Good Thing, Inc.
Cover design by Takeshi Takahashi
Cover printed by Yurchak Printing, Landisville, Penn.
Book printed and bound by Yurchak Printing, Landisville, Penn.
Date printed: April 2011

Printed in the United States of America

10 9 8 7 6 5 4 3 2 1

This book is printed on acid-free paper.

Contents

Foreword

Somewhere around fourth grade I decided that someday I was going to become a cop. It was the early 1970s, the women's movement was in full swing, and law enforcement seemed like it might lead to an exciting future for a farm girl from northern Illinois. I became a police dispatcher at age 17, foregoing my senior prom to work the night shift with no regrets, and that night I knew that law enforcement was definitely my future calling. I enrolled in a state university known for its criminal justice program and in 1980, at age 21, I was hired by a large Chicago suburb as a full time police officer. It was truly a dream come true: *I was a cop!!*

I did not realize it at the time, but I had not entered a profession: I had become part of a brotherhood, a culture, and a way of life. I was at the beginning of a 29-year walk down the warrior's path. I also did not know much about guns, tactics, or mindset—that would all come much later—but I did know that I wanted to put bad guys in jail, learn everything I could about criminal law, and make people who had been victimized feel safer. I wanted to make a difference. The police academy prepared me for the basics that I would need for field training. We learned how to shoot, to fight, to shine our shoes, to write reports—even how to deliver a baby (something that came in handy years later on patrol). We also learned how to become a team, how to protect each other, and how to protect ourselves. The academy staff seemed to spend an inordinate amount of time trying to frighten us, and they tested our physical strength as well as our internal fortitude; they needed to know if we had "the right stuff" to be real cops. Not all of us made it, and I was the only woman in my class to graduate. I was also the youngest, but I knew I was ready to fight crime.

After the academy, I was assigned to a field training officer (or "FTO") who would become a combination of teacher, parent, partner, and mentor. The FTO program was less formal in those days, but it was still a rookie's only way to make the transition from being a recruit candidate to a full-fledged police officer. I loved my FTO time; I was eager to learn and he was equally eager to teach, so we were a great team. In less than two years I became an investigator, and shortly after that I was assigned to a statewide narcotics task force where I would truly "grow up" as a cop. I learned how to write search warrants and cultivate informants. I began to study the science of officer survival and organizational communication. I battled my own cynicism even while fighting "the war on drugs," and I continued to revel in the adventure of police work.

When my time on the task force was over, I returned to patrol as an FTO: the student was now the trainer! I loved teaching recruits, and I became a classroom trainer as well. I went back into investigations and worked with kids, both offenders and victims, for several years before I was promoted to sergeant. As a sergeant in patrol, I supervised a patrol team, the K9 Unit, and the Animal Control Unit. I became a member of the Recruitment Team and the Honor Guard. As always, every day was fun and frustrating and exhilarating and exhausting.

I was later tasked with supervising my department's crime prevention unit. Initially hesitant because I could not imagine giving safety talks instead of chasing criminals, I now look back at my seven years in that unit as some of the most satisfying of my career. I became a bike patrol officer and an elderly services officer; I helped form our Citizen Police Academy and worked with our Community Radio Watch and other volunteer organizations. I also became a law enforcement author and began my television career with the Law Enforcement Television Network. Police work continued to open doors for me that I could not have imagined back in the academy. I was offered a lieutenant's position, turned it down, and then transferred back to patrol where I knew I wanted to finish out my final years as a cop. All the while I was expanding my "second" career as an author, trainer, and commentator. I retired in 2009, wearing my uniform for the last time on May 8th. My last call as a patrol sergeant was to assist in the foot pursuit of a teenage through the muddy back yards near our police station. Somehow that seemed to be a fitting final day.

Twenty-nine years as a police officer went by ridiculously fast. People always ask about my most memorable moments, but there are so many that it is difficult to single them out. They are not all happy, exciting moments, but they are ones I will never forget: I hid in a cornfield and arrested a murderer right before he stepped on me and my partner; I discovered a motel fire and began to evacuate the occupants before the firemen received the first call; I delivered a baby girl because her mom could not make it to the hospital in time; I helped a young girl escape from her sexually abusive father; I stood with my patrol team as we carried the casket of a good friend and fellow cop after his untimely death; I got shot at twice, I got hit by a car, I rescued baby ducks from a storm drain, and I did a thousand other things in between. I had a great career—No, I had an amazing adventure that happened to earn me a living.

Understand that no two days in police work are ever the same. The opportunities are endless, and the responsibilities are grave. If you choose law enforcement as a career, know that you are choosing to sacrifice, that you must have the moral courage to walk that warrior's path and do so righteously and properly. You will have powers and authority that none of your fellow citizens will have, and you must be able to live up to that great responsibility every day of your life, on or off duty. You will have to work hard to stay, physically and emotionally fit; this job can take its toll on us, on our families, and on our relationships. You will be the hunter and the hunted. You will be honored as well as cursed. You will not always be happy, but if you do it right, you will forever be satisfied that you chose this adventure above all others, that you chose to be a cop.

—Sergeant Betsy Brantner Smith (ret.)
HTTP://WWW.FEMALEFORCES.COM

Acknowledgments

Many thanks to Betsy, Rip, Beth, George, and Mary Ellen for protecting us for years and being willing to share, to Ann for her sharp eye and wit, and to Jim for a fun night of crime-busting.

Introduction

If you are reading this book, you are either contemplating a law enforcement career or already working in the law enforcement field. Maybe you are a city police officer or a sheriff's deputy and want to move up in your department. Maybe you see yourself working for one of the federal law enforcement agencies such as the U.S. Marshals Service or the Drug Enforcement Administration. Perhaps your interests lie in investigation of crimes, and you would like to be a police detective or work behind the scenes as a polygraph examiner or forensic scientist. Whichever your preference, this book can help.

How To Use This Book

This book is meant first to help you decide whether you want to pursue a career in law enforcement (if you are still in the contemplation stage), and then to help you go about pursuing it whether you are starting from scratch or already working in the field. The book covers the history of the law enforcement industry, the state of the industry today, how jobs are structured and fit together, tips for succeeding in law enforcement, how to talk like a pro even if you are not one, and resources for learning more.

The chapter "Industry History" describes the development of the law enforcement industry from the ancient times until the present day. For centuries, law enforcement was a family and individual matter, and there were almost no official law enforcement organizations. Early civilizations developed codes of laws to govern behavior and defined crimes and punishments, but there was no organized police force that maintained order. The English common law system came into being during the Middle Ages and eventually developed into a more formal system of law enforcement than had previously existed. European colonists brought their law enforcement practices with them to North America, and began appointing constables, justices of the peace, and sheriffs to preserve public safety. As cities grew bigger in the 1600s and 1700s they organized police forces and built small jails to house criminals. By the mid-1800s most cities had actual police forces. The practice of policing developed through the twentieth century and has been transformed by modern technology. This chapter concludes with interviews with a pair of retired New

Orleans police officers who share their experiences and perspectives on the way law enforcement work has changed. (Police dogs got bullet-proof vests before female officers got vests made for women!)

The chapter entitled "State of the Industry" contains statistics on the number of people working in the law enforcement industry in the United States, salary information, and prospects for growth. Law enforcement employs a fairly large number of people in the United States. Pay is moderate but steady, and most officers manage to increase it by working overtime and extra duty. The best pay is available in federal law enforcement. The work can be stressful and irregular, with long, odd hours and occasional stretches between jobs. Unions play a big role in some states, but not all states have law enforcement unions. There are numerous opportunities available at all levels of law enforcement throughout the United States; if you want to work in this field and have the necessary background, you should be able to find a job. This chapter also contains information on the organization of the law enforcement system, technology in areas such as forensics and weapons, and some facts about the criminal justice system. It concludes with an interview with a 41-year veteran. His advice? Plan to get a college degree, do not try to change the system too much, and become part of the community you serve.

Turn to "On the Job" to find out exactly what jobs exist within the law enforcement industry. This chapter describes the main positions from patrol officer to detective, explains who might do well in those jobs, and describes some paths of advancement within the industry.

"Tips for Success" will tell you how to find jobs and get ahead. It includes information on getting into police academies, thriving on the job, staying safe, passing tests to advance in the ranks, and getting into federal agencies. The main advice in this chapter? Pay your dues. (The interview subject in this chapter recommends that if you want to join a K9 unit you should put in some time as a quarry—which involves letting trainee dogs chase and bite you!) Landing plum assignments is often a matter of putting in the necessary time on the job. You cannot expect to be appointed to a SWAT team and make detective in your first week on a city police force, and desirable federal jobs usually go to people who have several years' experience working at local levels of law enforcement. College degrees help, too. Advancement in this profession comes from gaining experience and showing your competence through daily work and passing tests. There are no short cuts.

The law enforcement industry has its own language. Do you know what an "active shooter" is? What would you expect to find in a car with "K9" on it? If you have committed the crime of larceny, what did you do? Look to "Talk Like a Pro" to learn some of the jargon that you will have to know as a law enforcement professional.

Finally, the "Resources" chapter lists a number of Web sites and books that can help you on your way to a career in law enforcement. This book is only a start. There are many resources available in bookstores and online that can help you enter the profession, get ahead, and form valuable connections with colleagues.

The information in this book comes from a variety of sources—Web sites, books, online discussion boards, and conversations with current and former law enforcement personnel. By necessity, much of the information describes general situations; law enforcement organizations are very local, and every local jurisdiction has its own rules, procedures, and paths for advancement. You will learn the specifics that apply to your situation as you encounter them.

As you proceed in your career, you will gain much more information about the field from books, Web sites, and conversations, but most of your learning will be the result of experience. Law enforcement presents a vast scope for new experiences, growth, and personal satisfaction. Every day on the job will present challenges that have real impact on people's lives. Law enforcement is a vitally important field, and it takes a special type of person to succeed at it. Law enforcement officers must be brave, intelligent, and resourceful. If that describes you, you stand a good chance of thriving in law enforcement. Good luck, and stay safe.

Chapter 1

Industry History

For much of human history, law enforcement has been mainly the responsibility of individuals, families, and clans. Even in times and places with more evolved types of government and some public law enforcement, most crimes were handled as private matters. The concept of a public police force run by the government and paid for by tax dollars did not emerge until the 1600s. City police forces did not exist in most areas until the mid-1800s.

Ancient Law Enforcement

For thousands of years, law enforcement and public safety were mostly private matters. Family members disciplined one another for immoral or illicit acts. In Rome, for example, the father of the family was considered its absolute head, and had full power to discipline his family members for anything they did, up to and including killing them. A family that owned slaves had the right to discipline those slaves for their actions, whether or not those actions constituted crimes in the modern sense. If someone from outside a family committed a crime, the clan would band together to punish the offender.

Despite the fact that law enforcement was handled mainly by individuals and their relatives, people living in large cities saw early on the need for more formal systems of protecting public safety. Ancient inhabitants of the Middle East and Near East wrote some of the first legal codes. Greeks and Romans developed more elaborate systems of law enforcement.

Early Legal Codes

Some of the earliest known laws regulating criminal matters date from Babylon around 1760 B.C.E., when a king called Hammurabi created the Babylonian Empire in what is now Iraq. The Code of Hammurabi was carved on large pieces of stone designed to be displayed in temples so that people throughout the empire could refer to the laws written on it. Every major temple had its own copy. The Code established courts with judges who were given strict rules on how to make their decisions. Punishments were calibrated to the crimes that earned them: a person who injured another could be punished by having the same injury inflicted on him. This was a change from historical justice because it limited the retribution the victim's family would exact, and prevented feuds from escalating as various family members committed increasingly violent acts against their enemies. Those who disliked judges' initial decisions could appeal them, all the way to the king if necessary.

Fast
Facts

The Precepts of Sharia

Many Muslims around the world follow a body of laws called "Sharia" for regulating their daily lives. Americans most often hear the word "Sharia" in connection with stories about families and religious leaders inflicting discipline on individuals they believe have broken laws. Communities catch lawbreakers, and religious leaders impose sentences such as the amputation of the hands of thieves. Some of the more notorious cases of Sharia-based law enforcement include so-called "honor killings" of women caught in extramarital sexual relations. In these cases, women who have been caught in adultery or otherwise involved in sexual relations with men, willingly or not, are killed by their male relatives to preserve the honor of the family. Supporters of Sharia, however, point out that Sharia is generally a well-formulated and fair system of regulating community behavior. The majority of Sharia's precepts are actually concerned with nonviolent matters such as hygiene, diet and fasting, prayer, politics, and economics.

At about the same time, the Israelites west of Babylon introduced the body of laws known as the Ten Commandments. These laws provided a basic set of guidelines to govern society. Some of the commandments are still considered fundamental rules today; prohibitions against killing and theft are common in criminal laws everywhere. The Israelites also compiled a much more lengthy body of laws in the Old Testament book of Leviticus. Leviticus defines a number of acts that are considered wrong, including idolatry, fraud, sorcery, child sacrifice, and various types of sexual behavior, and prescribes punishments for these acts. Priests were put in charge of identifying law-breakers and seeing that they were punished.

Leviticus codified the principle of "an eye for an eye," which requires that a wrongdoer provide equitable compensation for the wrong he or she has done. Scholars have long debated whether this stricture would haven been taken literally, or if it simply meant that the punishment should be equivalent to the damage caused by the crime; certainly many people of many cultures have and still do apply the principle literally. For example, executing a murderer does the same thing to the murderer that the murderer did to his victim.

Greek and Roman Law Enforcement

Ancient Greece and Rome (500 B.C.E.–400 C.E.) had fairly elaborate systems of law enforcement, though much discipline still took place within the privacy of the family or was handled through feuds and vendettas. Athens, for example, maintained a body of public slaves called the Scythian Archers that served as a police force. They arrested criminals, guarded prisons, and maintained order at public meetings. They appear to have performed crowd control at markets and other public events, removing drunks and whipping disorderly men.

During the Roman Republic (510 B.C.E.–27 B.C.E.), elected officials called aediles were in charge of preserving public order, organizing public festivals, and maintaining public buildings. Aediles took on many of the responsibilities of modern law enforcement organizations: They regulated traffic, removed dangerous animals, arrested gamblers and loan sharks, watched over behavior in taverns and public baths, registered prostitutes and brothels, and guarded public morals in general. They oversaw the use of public land, and prevented any one individual from exploiting too great a share of public resources such as grazing land. During a span the Roman Empire (27 B.C.E–14 C.E.), the city of Rome was divided in 14 wards, each protected by large forces of men. The emperor himself was protected by a group of bodyguards called the Praetorian Guard. These guards patrolled the palace and major city buildings, but their primary duty was to protect the ruling family, not public order.

Romans had many methods of disciplining wrongdoers. Flogging and fines were common punishments for ordinary crimes. Those who committed treason or murder might be executed by being flung off a cliff called the Tarpeian Rock or by being strangled in a pit called the Tullianum. Slaves who committed crimes were sometimes executed by crucifixion—hung on crosses or stakes and left until they died. The Romans sometimes broke the legs of crucified criminals to make them die faster; without this additional measure, a crucifixion victim could hang for days before dying.

Medieval European Law Enforcement

During the medieval and early modern periods (about 400–1700 C.E.), European societies developed more complex bodies of laws, leading up to modern law enforcement principles. However, most law enforcement was still done by individuals rather than the state. Families and clans were the most important social grouping, and took care of handling crimes against family members. The Catholic Church also took on some responsibility for maintaining public safety and public morality. "Crimes" were not only acts that harmed others; they also included acts that were immoral and could put a person's immortal soul in jeopardy.

Celtic Family Feuds and Laws

The Celtic peoples of ancient and medieval Europe organized themselves by clans, and clans took on most of the burden of law enforcement. If a Celtic man was insulted or murdered by someone from another clan, his kinsmen would all assume the responsibility of avenging him. This resulted in extended feuds between families throughout the Celtic world. Blood feuds could devastate families because they could precipitate never-ending cycles of murder; when a person was killed, his or her family felt obligated to kill the murderer. The murderer's family would then feel compelled to kill the murderer's murderer, and so on for years if necessary.

In order to bring these destructive feuds in line, Celtic societies created a body of laws that forced murderers to compensate the families of their victims. The idea was that monetary compensation would effectively end the feud, allowing the rival clans to resume peaceful relations and stop killing one another. Historians believe these laws originated among European Celtic peoples during the Bronze Age, between 2300 and 900 b.c.e. The Brehon laws of Ireland are one of the best-known examples. These laws were not written down. Instead Celtic legal experts memorized the body of laws so that they could interpret them and resolve disputes.

Under Celtic law, every crime merited a specific compensation; cutting off someone's hand earned a smaller payment to the victim than murdering someone. If a person harmed another, the victim or the victim's family would bring the case before a chief and a legal expert. The legal expert would listen to the facts and decide the appropriate punishment. There were several levels of court. Petty disputes went to the courts of local chiefs, while major disputes might go all the way to a king. A party who brought a case to court had to bring at least two witnesses to testify on his behalf. Social rank was important in courts. A person of lower rank could not always testify against someone of higher class. Social rank also determined which crimes were prosecuted and how they were punished. Criminals were almost never sentenced to death. The only exception to this rule was when a murderer failed to pay the full amount of the specified fine, in which case he might be executed. Celtic kings and chiefs might occasionally have criminals hanged or drowned, but they did this on their own authority, outside that of the Celtic courts.

Germanic Law Enforcement

The German peoples who lived in central and northern Europe in ancient and medieval times also organized themselves by clans and tribes, with blood relationships the most important tie among people. For almost all of the ancient period they governed themselves according to custom, passed orally from generation to generation. These laws specified the treatment of criminals and the settlement of disputes. Germanic tribes did not begin to compile formal legal codes until the very end of the Roman Empire.

Germanic laws covered many different types of crime. Stealing cattle was a serious offense, and penalties varied depending on the value of the cattle stolen; a bull owned by the king merited a higher fine than a bull that serviced only the cows of a single herd owned by an ordinary man. Stealing an object that lay outside a house was not as serious as breaking into a house to steal something. Merely breaking into a house without stealing anything was also a crime, especially if the thief broke a lock to get in. Rape, assault, insult, and murder were all criminal offenses punishable by fines. There were no prisons or incarceration in the modern sense. Tribes set fines according to the value of the victim. Killing a pregnant woman merited a higher fine than killing a woman past her childbearing years. If a murderer concealed his victim in an attempt to hide his crime, the punishment was greater than if he did not. A murderer who did not have enough money to pay the fine was expected to ask his relatives and friends for help. If he still could not raise enough money, he might be executed. Priests played an important part in determining crimes and punishments, which could include reprimands or flogging.

Northern European Law Enforcement

Medieval Norse countries all used a law enforcement system that combined public and private efforts. Iceland, for example, was divided into four quarters. The inhabitants of each quarter elected an official called a lawspeaker every three years. The lawspeaker would memorize the laws so that he could preside over the legislature and give legal advice. Lawspeakers would occasionally recite all the laws; anyone interested in researching a legal point had to come hear the lawspeaker to know what was allowed. The legislature passed laws regulating criminal matters. These laws were applied by a system of courts, ranging from small private courts arranged on an ad-hoc basis to deal with specific conflicts, to courts at the quarter level, to the national assembly, which met once a year. Any case that was undecided could move up to the next higher level of court.

The prosecution of a crime was the business of the victim or his or her family. The state did not prosecute crimes itself. A victim could settle a matter privately with the offender without resorting to courts at all. If a case went to court, the individuals each presented their case, calling witnesses if necessary. The men sitting on the court would decide the defendant's guilt or innocence by majority vote. Punishments were almost always fines, which were determined by the magnitude of the crime. A person who killed another person would pay the victim's family a sum of money called "wergild," which means, "man money."

The main exception to the rule of paying fines was in the case of murderers who did not follow acceptable procedures after killing. According to Icelandic law, someone who killed a man was required to announce this fact to his neighbors within three days. If he did not do this, he would be considered a murderer and could be made an outlaw. An outlaw could not enter society without being caught and punished harshly, so outlaws were forced to live in the wilderness on their own.

There were some disadvantages to this system. A victim too poor or friendless to negotiate with the offender or bring a lawsuit would not be able to seek vindication. The Norse people dealt with this problem by allowing a victim to sell his or her case to someone else, who could then prosecute it and collect compensation from the offender. Rich people could sometimes commit crimes with impunity, but for the most part the monetary penalty for killing served as an effective deterrent. Occasionally a court's decision was based more on the power and influence of one of the parties than the actual facts of the matter.

Anglo-Saxons and English Common Law

English common law, which forms the main basis for the American legal system, developed out of Germanic and Norse legal traditions. Germanic law arrived in the British Isles when a Germanic people called the Anglo-Saxons sailed to England from Germany and Denmark during the 400s and quickly dominated the Celtic locals. In creating their legal system, the Anglo-Saxons were influenced by Roman law, Christian principles, and their own Germanic traditions. During the medieval period, law enforcement was performed by various groups: individual families, local and regional lords, and the Catholic Church all took care of various aspects of law enforcement.

Anglo-Saxons emphasized loyalty—to one's own lord, to the king, to the Church, and most especially to one's family. They took oaths extremely seriously. Violence was apparently a major problem, if literature of the period is to be believed, and the Anglo-Saxon legal system was designed to maintain order. All freemen took an oath at the age of 12, swearing to abstain from and denounce all major crimes. Anyone who committed a crime had not only done a wrong act, he had also broken his oath, which was considered an act of disloyalty to the community. A criminal did not just bring opprobrium upon himself, but upon his whole family, and the entire family could be punished for a crime committed by one of its members.

Around 600 c.e., the Anglo-Saxons broke with their older tradition of transmitting all laws orally and began putting laws into writing when King Ethelbert of Kent issued the first known written legal code in England. This code listed crimes and their accompanying fines. The worst punishments were reserved for crimes against Church property or priests. Ethelbert's code was followed by a number of other written legal codes produced over the next four centuries by kings and their councils. These codes probably were not new laws, but simply written versions of rules that Germanic peoples had used for centuries.

The Anglo-Saxons set up a series of courts throughout the land, with major courts in each shire and borough and smaller local courts known as "hundred" courts. The king appointed officials to preside over these courts. The officials of hundred courts, assisted by the families of victims, would track down accused criminals and bring them back to the courts to hear the cases against them.

In court, the victim would state his charge and the defendant would answer it. The defendant would often respond simply by swearing that he had not committed the crime in question, and would call upon friends to swear that his oath was true. If his friends did so, the defendant would go free. Some historians believe this system worked mainly because the population attending a hundred court was small, the individuals all knew one another and had to live together, and were not likely to lie. A defendant who was known to be guilty would be unable to find supporters to swear that his oath was true, and would probably be found guilty.

The Beginnings of Formal Law Enforcement

Around 1100, English towns began to employ constables, officials specifically charged with keeping the peace. Constables guarded property, especially weapons, and generally tried to keep crime down. Constables were not the only law enforcement officials; in fact almost anyone was allowed to stop crimes and arrest lawbreakers. The constable's main duty was to record events and if necessary to arrest lawbreakers, but he did not have the authority to determine guilt or innocence or set their punishments, which were the responsibility of a judge. The constable thus had a major role in gathering evidence for use in court. Parishes and villages throughout England used constables well into the nineteenth century.

In 1195, King Richard I of England appointed knights called "keepers of the peace" to preserve the peace in areas plagued by crime and lawlessness. In the 1300s, the English government created a number of justices of the peace who were appointed to maintain law in every county. Justices of the peace were authorized to arrest and imprison lawbreakers in order to keep them from causing more trouble before they could be tried and sentenced. They also conducted trials for minor offenses. Justices of the peace, like constables, were usually unpaid. Consequently, the offices were most often held by landed gentry who did not need to spend all their time working.

Medieval Punishments

Medieval punishments did not as a rule include long-term imprisonment. For the most part, lawbreakers were punished quickly and often quite harshly. Anglo-Saxon punishments, for example, included fines, physical mutilation such as branding or chopping off a limb, execution, or exile. Sometimes a criminal's entire family would be punished. Capital punishment was not the rule, but was common enough that around 930 King Aethelstan raised the age of criminal responsibility from 12 to 16 because he thought it was too cruel to execute young people for crimes such as stealing sheep.

Torture was considered an acceptable part of law enforcement during the Middle Ages and well into the modern era. It became quite common in England during the reign of Henry VIII and Elizabeth I, and was regularly used during the Spanish Inquisition. Torture had several purposes. It could break the victim's will and force him or her to confess to crimes. The fact that many confessions were outlandish and impossible did not convince torturers that their methods were ineffective. It could serve as a punishment in its own right. It was an excellent means of intimidating other groups, which was why rulers often used it on political enemies.

Acts that most people today would consider torture included stretching a person on a rack, attaching a person to a large wheel and breaking his bones, boiling a victim alive in either water or oil,

Problem Solving

Persecuting Witchcraft

What do you do if it is 1570 and your children are sick, your cattle are dying, your well has dried up, and you have no idea why? You blame it on a witch, of course! Witchcraft was one of the most pressing public safety concerns in the sixteenth and seventeenth centuries. Lacking an understanding of the natural world and effective medicine, people often assumed that their misfortunes were caused by witches acting in league with the devil. Law enforcement officials investigated accusations of witchcraft; arrested accused witches; housed them in jails, sheds, or houses; and prosecuted cases against them, using torture as necessary to elicit confessions. People found guilty of witchcraft were often executed by hanging or burning. The Salem Witch Trials that took place in Massachusetts in 1692–93 were the most infamous American trials, but they pale in comparison to witch prosecution in Europe, where thousands of people were executed for witchcraft.

cutting or burning off a woman's breasts, plucking out eyes, and various other unpleasant acts. Someone who committed treason might be hanged, drawn, and quartered, which involved being dragged to a place of execution, hanged by the neck until nearly dead, disemboweled while still alive, and then cut into four pieces that could be displayed in different locations. Lesser crimes might earn a session sitting in the pillory or stocks—devices designed to immobilize the perpetrator in a humiliating and uncomfortable posture subject to jeers and mistreatment from spectators.

The Development of Modern Law Enforcement

By the time Europeans began to colonize North America, the English criminal justice system was fairly well developed. Other European nations used similar systems combining public, private, and religious law enforcement. Europeans who settled in North America brought their systems with them, though it took many years for formal law enforcement to become widespread throughout the continent.

Early Rudimentary North American Law Enforcement Systems

As towns and cities grew, they appointed constables, justices of the peace, and sheriffs much the way European cities had. These officers responded to complaints and investigated crimes; they also collected taxes, ran elections, and handled various other matters of business. County sheriffs and other officials were typically paid little for their work, which made them less than enthusiastic about spending too much time on law enforcement and prone to corruption. Individual settlers still took much of the responsibility for defending themselves or handling other crimes against themselves or their families.

The first formal law enforcement office in the future United States was the New York City Sheriff's Office, which was founded in 1626. In the 1630s the city of Boston founded its Night Watch, which used officers to patrol city streets at night. Patrolmen carried rattles to sound the alarm and long hooked poles, which they could use to grab running criminals. New Orleans organized militia patrols in the early 1800s, supplementing them with vigilante committees.

In the early days of law enforcement in North America, prisons were small and set up for temporary housing of prisoners awaiting trial. They were not especially secure, and prisoners could escape easily. Overcrowding became a serious problem as populations grew. Though jailers received county funds to care for their charges, they were as tempted as sheriffs to embezzle, to accept bribes, and to engage in illegal acts such as selling whiskey to inmates.

The Wild West

The U.S. Marshals were established in 1789 as part of the Judicial Department outlined in the Articles of Constitution. President George Washington and the first Congress believed that fair administration of justice and enforcement of laws were essential to the stability of the new nation. The U.S. marshals were essential for preserving order. Most of the first marshals had already served in the American Revolution, so they had ample experience with weapons, combat, and military leadership. They were put in charge of the enforcement of federal laws, including arresting and handling federal prisoners, issuing warrants, summonses, and subpoenas, and swearing in temporary troops of men to help them hunt lawbreakers. These groups of men assembled to go after felons were known as *posses*. The marshals were also given the job of renting courtrooms, hiring clerks,

INTERVIEW

The Rise of the Female Officer

Mary Ellen Grace
Louisiana Gaming Commission, New Orleans Police Department

What law enforcement jobs have you held?

I started out as a special agent with the Louisiana Gaming Commission in New Orleans. Governor Foster abolished my entire 96-person unit in 1995. I then became a probation and parole agent and served simultaneously as a reserve officer in the New Orleans Police Department.

How did you get into law enforcement?

As a young girl in the 1960s, I was a daddy's girl. Instead of being in the kitchen learning to cook, I would watch *Dragnet* with my dad, and I think I inherited an interest in law enforcement from him. He even helped me fill out a job application for the FBI, but I didn't have my degree at the time so that didn't work.

I did everything sort of backwards. Most people start as police officers first and go to college on state funds. I paid for my own college and then became an officer. I started out studying business at Dominican College. I needed a couple of electives so I took some criminal justice courses to complete my degree. I realized I was totally infatuated with my criminal justice classes. I finished my business degree and then transferred over to Tulane, and I think I only needed 34 more credits to get a second BA in criminal justice. Then I had to go through the police academy to get a job as a special agent.

What was law enforcement like when you got started ?

It was still very, very sexist when I started in the 1980s. You had desk personnel that mysteriously couldn't find the key to the lady's room so you'd have to go to a coffee shop six blocks away. Or if you were working on a legitimate project, they could never find paper for the Xerox machine, to stall you and maybe hope that you would miss a deadline. Then you would get the snotty little comments like, "Why aren't you home pregnant and cooking?" The department didn't put first names on name tags, so guys would think you were a man, and when you showed up at a new unit, they might say "Oh, Christ, they sent me a woman." The whole NOPD was only 11 percent women in 1989. Sometimes it seems that only one girl graduated per academy class—they would mysteriously flunk them out.

In recent years women have been able to get promoted—there are women sergeants and even captains now. I think the federal government's anti-discrimination policies were the only salvation for women in law enforcement. I don't think they would ever have been welcomed with open arms if the federal government had not done that. Right now today, there are still only two captains who are women out of about 30 or 40 captains total.

I personally was a bit offended when the department started mandating bullet-proof vests—the guys got their vests, the dogs got their vests, and the women were last. And I love dogs! But that's where the priorities were. They wouldn't buy women's vests because they cost a bit more. They tried to squeeze us into men's vests until a couple of the more mouthy women just refused to wear them and demanded women's vests.

What differences do you see between law enforcement then and now?
I think work is much more dangerous now than it used to be. I have never thought of myself as having a strong personality or strong command presence. I think that I hid behind the uniform, and let the uniform speak for me. That's not doable today. The criminals just shoot at you, you're just like target practice for them now. There's no respect for the uniform anymore and they would probably get great pleasure in provoking you so that you violate their civil rights.

I've seen a real change in the attitudes of officers over the past 20 of 30 years. The guys who went through the academy in the 1970s had fun there and on the job. I had some fun, but not as much. With the people going through now, you would think they were at a wake. There is no liveliness in their voices. It's like a sour, somber mood has taken over and there is no light-heartedness or laughter. They all look like robots out there—their heads shaved, no room for individuality. I think the weight of the seriousness will affect them. It could ruin your career, because you've got to be young and energetic. You need too much energy to put up with the foolishness, and if you take away the high-spiritedness of the personality, I don't know.

What sort of situations have you handled?
You encounter a nice variety of criminals in New Orleans. I remember a little 5-year-old boy putting his hands on his hips and cocking his head and telling me to take him to his mother to get her to sign the papers for him—he knew the system well enough to know that his mother was responsible for kids under 9 years old. Each type of criminal contributes their two cents equally—domestic violence is a very serious issue, drug dealing, truancy, prostitution.

(continues on next page)

INTERVIEW

The Rise of the Female Officer (continued)

Then there are car thieves, which are divided into two types —the thief that wants the car intact or for parts, and joy riders who steal cars in order to be initiated into a gang. If you want to get into a gang, you have six or seven hours at night to steal a certain number of cars, drive them, and park them. This is how you prove that you're a man and capable of joining these particular street gangs. For girls, they have to shoplift a certain dollar amount of merchandise from a mall in order to be initiated into the gangs. Sometimes the girls are even worse than the guys.

bailiffs, judges, and attorneys, scheduling trials, and making sure that prisoners, jurors, and witnesses were present when trials began. In the West, deputy marshals served as the federal government's representatives in their areas. They hunted down outlaws, protected legal businesses, and took the census.

Marshals, sheriffs, and other officers were responsible for catching suspected criminals and bringing them back to town. There the suspects would be placed in custody, typically in a small town jail, to await trial in front of a judge and possibly a jury. Frontier judges often were untrained in the law, and some new towns had no courthouses, forcing judges to hold trials in other buildings such as saloons. Lawyers were also few and far between, as were jurors, especially in regions that were not yet fully settled.

Local sheriffs and marshals did not always work alone. They had the authority to conscript local men to help them pursue criminals; this power was known as *posse comitatus*, a medieval Latin expression referring to the power to enforce the law. During the nineteenth century, marshals were often required to catch fugitive slaves and return them to their owners; they were allowed to muster posses of civilian men to help them with this task. A man who refused to help a marshal hunt slaves could be heavily fined and imprisoned.

Despite the presence of marshals and sheriffs, frontier areas tended to be fairly lawless well into the nineteenth century. There were not nearly enough law enforcers to cover their large territories, the inhabitants of which were often rambunctious and not inclined to respect laws. They were not paid very much for their work. If a wrongdoer resisted arrest, they could not do much about it, as there were few legal penalties for this act. They gradually gained some assistance in the form of county sheriffs and other local officers, but all of these individuals faced the same problems of too much work, too little pay, and an abundance of lawbreakers. Civilian settlers typically had to defend themselves from thieves and other

On the Cutting Edge

Killing the Condemned

Civilized people have struggled for centuries with a dilemma: How can one execute a convicted criminal in a way that causes the victim the smallest amount of suffering? Hanging, popular for the past two millennia, can be very effective when done correctly. Unfortunately, a botched hanging can either slowly strangle a victim or rip his head off, both unappealing. Firing squads were common in the 19th and early twentieth century; they are quick but loud and require many shooters. Gas chambers, used during the first half of the twentieth century, cause convulsions. Electric chairs sometimes set victims on fire. The guillotine was invented in the late 1700s to decapitate people in more efficiently than earlier methods, such as hacking away at the neck with an axe. Designed by a committee including a professor of anatomy and a harpsichord maker, it was cutting-edge technology for its time.

Thirty-seven U.S. states allow capital punishment today. Although a few states still technically allow hanging and electrocution, most use lethal injection, which uses ultra-fast-acting barbiturates to stop the heart of the victim. Lethal injection looks very peaceful, though some critics contend that it is actually quite painful. Experts have been working on new drug combinations to avoid any discomfort to victims.

INTERVIEW

Connections Make a Career

George Wichser
New Orleans Police Department, Retired

How did you get into law enforcement?
My first introduction to law enforcement was with the Louisiana National Guard military police in 1970. I was selected for the 39th MP [Military Police] company. I went to military training and learned the federal government system, and then came back home to New Orleans. I knew several police officers from my days in the MP company. My experience and my association with those fine gentlemen helped me get a job, and I ended up joining the New Orleans Police Department in 1975.

What was law enforcement like when you got started?
The first hurdle I had to cross was the police academy, which was 17 weeks. Once I completed that, the sergeant of the tactical riot squad of the NOPD, knowing that I was militarily trained, approached me and asked if I wanted to be assigned to that unit. Of course I said yes because I didn't particularly want to go to the district. I stayed in the tactical unit for five years and then got an opportunity to ride motorcycles and write traffic tickets and work escorts. I stayed there for a number of years. Then I was able to move into the hit and run investigations of motor vehicles. And then from there I moved to automobile fatality investigations and stayed there a number of years. I retired after 27 years on the police force.

I took a hiatus for one year, and then went to Tulane University and joined their police force. I was able to work there for four years until I came down with a liver problem. Of course the doctor put me on disability and I can't work anymore.

wrongdoers, and the concept of "frontier justice" was well accepted by most people living in newly settled areas.

The Beginning of City Police Forces

The concept of a police force organized by the government and paid for out of taxpayer funds was a new one that emerged in France in the eighteenth century. The rise of modern police forces goes along

What differences do you see between law enforcement then and now?

Different policing techniques have been introduced, especially a style of policing that started in Greensboro, North Carolina, called community policing. This meant that if you concentrate your police efforts on the community problems, the criminal problems will be taken care of because the population will be friendlier to the police—it would be a different response. The chief in Greensboro has had pretty good success with it.

Officers are more afraid that they'll get in trouble if they use force in making arrests. I'll be honest, there will always be corruption in a lot of places. The police department had its corruption. But years ago the superintendent didn't make a big deal out of it in that he didn't parade these people before the public. He just walked them out the backdoor and they were gone; he fired them. Now, if you're found to be corrupt, you're paraded in the paper, prosecuted. What that's done is that the officers and the rank and file aren't as willing to take a chance in their law enforcement. If you do something during an arrest that you think is okay, the police department may decide it's a crime and end up prosecuting you for it.

What about minorities?

Now there are more black officers than white officers. The white officers have mostly left because they felt that they were discriminated against. When I started, a very small proportion of the police force was black. Those black officers worked as tow-truck drivers, picking up automobiles and working at the auto pound. There were maybe five or six officers who were allowed to work in good assignments, such as detective, but only because those officers were very knowledgeable of the criminal element in the city so they would know a lot. Black officers entered the force in 1964 but entered the force in real numbers in the 1980s. The first black superintendent came on in the 1980s.

with the rise of the modern state, which occurred from the late 1700s (with the American and French Revolutions) and continued through the 1800s.

Cities began to create police forces in the 1800s. Richmond, Virginia, claims one of the nation's first police forces. The Richmond Police Department was founded in 1807, followed by the construction of the city's first jail in 1816. The Boston Day Police was established in 1838 (the Night Watch still existed) and the New York City

Police Department in 1844. In 1854, the Boston Police Department was founded, combining the Night Watch and the Day Police into one organization. Officers in Boston gave up their old hooks and replaced them with short clubs that they used to beat wrongdoers into submission. Other major cities followed suit with their own city police departments. Chicago founded its department in 1855. New Orleans consolidated its police force and created a chief of police in 1852.

Corruption was a common problem with nineteenth century police forces. Many individuals did not actually want the police to stop all crime; gambling, prostitution, alcohol sales, and other types of organized crime were too profitable for their proponents to give up. Because police officers were paid little, it was easy to bribe them to ignore crimes. Officers found it difficult to arrest their friends or family members. Police departments were funded by government money, so it was difficult for them to resist political pressure to handle or fail to handle certain matters. The office of police chief was especially highly politicized. Officers were almost exclusively white men, who were often unwilling to assist minority or female crime victims. Most departments did not train their officers, so enforcement of laws could be idiosyncratic. Not surprisingly, crime thrived in big cities despite the presence of police.

Federal and State Jurisdiction

The United States has always struggled with balancing federal and state law enforcement. Until the late nineteenth century, law enforcement was almost always considered the responsibility of state and local governments. This changed in 1886 when the U.S. Supreme Court in the case *Wabash v. Illinois* found that the federal government was responsible for interstate law enforcement. This news forced the Justice Department to provide officers who could investigate interstate crimes. In 1908, President Theodore Roosevelt created an organization called the Bureau of Investigation, staffed by 12 agents from the Secret Service. These agents initially worked on interstate prostitution. In 1933 the organization was renamed the Division of Investigation and attached to the Bureau of Prohibition, which enforced anti-alcohol policies. In 1935 it was finally named the Federal Bureau of Investigation (FBI) and placed under the leadership of J. Edgar Hoover.

Hoover built the FBI into a large and well-funded organization that investigated some of the most significant crimes in the United States, including organized crime and the work of the Ku Klux Klan. The FBI then worked in international espionage during the Second World War, the investigation of John F. Kennedy's assassination in the sixties, the Oklahoma City Bombing in the nineties, and other major crimes.

State police were initially created to oversee labor disputes. The first state police agency was established in Pennsylvania in 1905. The state legislature created the state police in response to a mine strike in 1902; critics claimed that the new state police force had been founded to repress organized labor, while supporters countered that the company's own police force had been more repressive to unions. New York State created its own police force in 1917, also to handle labor disputes and union problems. As the twentieth century progressed, labor issues became less of a problem for most states, and state police forces moved their attention to the newly built interstate highways and automobiles, enforcing traffic laws, attending accidents, and pursuing criminals who used the highways for criminal purposes such as transporting drugs.

Professional
Ethics

Abuses of Power

J. Edgar Hoover was notorious for his practice of using wiretaps and hidden microphones to record private conversations among people not accused of crimes and then maintaining files on his subjects that he could use to blackmail them. He sought out individuals that he believed were "subversive" to the U.S. government, including supposed communists and civil rights activists. Hoover's papers, which were released in 2007, revealed that he had kept records on over 12,000 Americans, and had suggested to President Truman that they all be arrested. Modern historians and politicians believe that Hoover abused his power and made the most of his nearly 50 years as director of the Bureau to achieve his own ends. Since Hoover's day, FBI directors have been limited to 10-year terms.

Private security forces have co-existed with state-sponsored law enforcement for hundreds of years. In the days before effective state police forces existed, private law enforcement was the only way many people could stop crime. Companies and wealthy individuals would arrange for protection of their property and themselves and pay directly for this service. The railroad companies of the nineteenth century created their own law enforcement forces to protect trains and passengers passing through unpopulated areas. Cities may also subcontract law enforcement duties to private companies. For example, in 1946 San Francisco passed a law creating the Patrol Special Police Force, a private company that contracted for law enforcement services beyond those that the city provided. Even today, many businesses pay for their own security personnel, many of whom have legal status as state law enforcement officers. For example, in South Carolina, private security officers have the same enforcement authority as Sheriff's Deputies.

Modernization of Police Work

Up until about 1900, police technology was fairly straightforward. Officers patrolled on foot or on horseback. Criminals might be transported in wagons or trains if they had to cover a long distance. Communication was done by letter, by telegraph, or in person. Officers carried revolvers and short clubs, supplementing their arsenals with rifles or shotguns for long-range shots. Anyone who wanted immediate police assistance had to speak in person to an officer.

All of this changed in the early 1900s with the invention of the automobile, the radio, and the telephone. For the first time, victims of crimes could call police and expect a quick response. Around the same time, police departments became more professional. Police chiefs such as John M. Glass of the Los Angeles Police Department (LAPD), who served from 1889 to 1900, introduced military-style uniforms and weapons, organized districts, substations, and patrols, and set requirements for entry-level officers. Departments began training their officers in the 1910s.

August Vollmer, who in 1905 became chief of the police in Berkeley, California, is considered by many to be the father of modern law enforcement. He read numerous European treatises on criminal justice and psychology, and applied what he learned to his police force. He introduced innovations such as the use of blood, soil, and fiber sample analysis in detective work, lie detector tests, fingerprinting, and squad cars equipped with two-way radios. He created an efficient record-keeping system that streamlined investigations. Requiring officers to adhere to a strict code of conduct, he established a school of criminology in 1916 and required his officers to attend classes. His officers also had to practice marksmanship.

Vollmer's protégé O.W. Wilson studied at Berkeley and worked as a police officer on the force there during the 1920s. He became chief of the Wichita Police Department in 1928 and spent the next decade reforming the department to make officers more professional and reduce corruption. He required new officers to have a college education, and he followed Vollmer's example of putting two-way radios in squad cars both to facilitate communication and to allow better supervision of patrol officers. He introduced the use of a mobile crime laboratory.

Wilson later moved to Chicago in 1960 and reformed the police department there. His reforms in Chicago included the creation of a non-partisan police board, the redrawing of police districts without consideration of politics, increasing discipline, requiring higher standards for new hires, using computers to keep records, and replacing foot patrols with patrols done in squad cars. He deliberately recruited African Americans to work as officers and promoted some black officers to the rank of sergeant in an effort to improve race relations. Wilson believed that rapid response to calls and regular patrols were the key to effective law enforcement because they showed criminals that the police were always present. Wilson's work was the basis for most law enforcement practices until quite recently.

Community Policing
In the 1990s, police departments began to supplement regular patrols with "community policing," a practice in which police collaborate with community members to reduce local crime. In the 1960s and 70s, certain communities felt themselves to be at odds with police. Taking officers off the beat and putting them in cars isolated them from the communities they patrolled, which meant they no longer got to know individual community members.

Community policing attempts to put officers back into communities, where they can gather essential information and stop crimes before they occur. It also encourages community residents to participate in crime prevention efforts by telling police of criminal activity and identifying lawbreakers. Community residents can meet with officers on a regular basis to discuss problems, including crimes as well as complaints about police. Greensboro, North Carolina, began an experimental community policing program in 1989, with notable success. Chicago implemented its community policing program in 1993, and other cities followed. So far the method seems to be quite effective at slowing crime.

Women and Minorities

Women did not enter law enforcement in significant numbers until well into the twentieth century. During the 1800s, cities hired women to work as matrons in prisons, taking care of female prisoners, but women did not patrol the streets. The first female police officer in the United States was Alice Stebbins Wells, a former social worker who became a policewoman in the Los Angeles Police Department in 1910. Her responsibilities included supervising dance halls, skating rinks, cinemas, and other places of recreation where children and women congregated. She was especially useful for questioning young girls and rendering aid to female crime victims. Wells actively promoted the need to hire more female officers, emphasizing the qualifications of women to work with juveniles and female criminals. Because of her work, the LAPD and other police departments across the country began hiring more female police officers.

Women remained a small portion of most police forces through the twentieth century. Up until the 1950s, women officers were restricted to duties involving women and juveniles and were not given plum field assignments. They were very rarely promoted to ranks above sergeant, and many police departments did not order equipment that could fit women. Big changes began with the passage of the Civil Rights Act of 1964, a federal law that prohibits discrimination by employers on the basis of race, color, religion, sex, or national origin. In the 1980s lawsuits and feminist pressure forced many departments to hire more women and treat them equally with male officers, but this profession is still overwhelmingly male. Women today make up only about 16 percent of all police officers nationwide (though some departments have a much higher percentage of female officers), and the percentage of women serving as police lieutenants and captains is even smaller.

Police forces were overwhelmingly white throughout most of the twentieth century. In the Northeast, Irish men came to dominate police departments back in the mid–1800s, after the large influx of Irish immigrants fleeing the potato famine of the 1840s. By the

1860s, about half of the police officers in New York and Boston were Irish-Americans. This state of affairs continued well into the twentieth century; in the 1970s, a large proportion of Boston's police still identified themselves as Irish-Americans.

The LAPD hired two black officers in 1886, making it the first department in the country to do so. Other departments gradually hired minorities, somewhat influenced by the Civil Rights Act of 1964 which forbade employment discrimination on the basis of race, but it was not until the 1980s and 1990s that departments began hiring minorities in any real numbers. Police departments gradually began to see that the racial composition of their forces was causing community relations problems; racial minorities often felt that they were unfairly treated by white officers. Departments implemented hiring quotas in an effort to increase the number of minority officers on their forces. Subsequent research revealed that the presence of minority officers seemed to have an actual deterrent effect on violent crime in those officers' neighborhoods. As of 1990, only 30 percent of police officers nationwide were minorities; this percentage had increased to 38 percent by 2000. Few minority officers were promoted to higher ranks such as lieutenant or captain during the twentieth century. On the other hand, in some major cities such as Atlanta and Detroit, black officers represented a majority of the force by 1993, and New York, Los Angeles, Chicago, and Houston have all had black police chiefs.

Hispanic populations have increased dramatically in the United States in the past few decades. As of 2008, there were nearly 47 million Hispanic people living in the United States, about 15 percent of the total population. The Hispanic population grew 3.2 percent between 2007 and 2008, making Hispanics the fastest-growing minority group in the country. The U.S. Census Bureau predicts that the Hispanic population will be nearly 133 million by 2050, at which point Hispanics will constitute 30 percent of the population. So far, numbers of Hispanic police officers have not kept pace with general population trends. As of the late 1900s, many police departments had no Spanish-speaking officers on their forces. Some cities have been reversing this trend, though. Los Angeles was nearly all white and Protestant when the LAPD was founded in 1949. In the 1980s, the force was still 80 percent white. In 2000, one third of the force was Hispanic or Latino, close to the population proportion. By 2007, nearly half of Los Angeles' population was Hispanic or Latino, with sizable Asian minorities, especially Koreans, Philippinos, and

Chinese. In 2009, the LAPD was 42 percent Latino, 7 percent Asian, 12 percent black, and 37 percent white, fairly close to the city's demographic profile.

Race relations have been a big problem for law enforcement forces for many years. Lynching, the capture and execution of black people by mobs throughout the 1800s and well into the twentieth century, was often done with the cooperation of local law enforcement officers. Racial differences have often played a role in incidents of police brutality. In 1991 LAPD officers beat a black man named Rodney King after he resisted arrest; the violence of the beating, captured on video by a bystander, precipitated a surge of racially based anger. A year later the officers involved in the beating were acquitted of wrongdoing, which triggered the six-day 1992 Los Angeles Riots. In 1997, New York City police assaulted Haitian immigrant Abner Louima while he was in custody, triggering protests by minority communities in New York City. Analyses of police brutality over the past several decades typically have found that the actual incidence of police brutality is greater than reported because victims have historically been unwilling to come forward with accusations. Amnesty International reports that brutality is still common in U.S. prisons.

A Brief Chronology

c. 1760 B.C.E.: Hammurabi's code is established.

c. 500 B.C.E.–400 C.E.: Greeks in Athens institute the Scythian Archers, one of the world's first known police forces.

27 B.C.E.–14 C.E.: Rome divided into 14 wards, a forerunner to the modern precinct system.

400–1000: Gradual development of English Common Law.

c. 600: King Ethelbert of Kent issues written legal code.

1100: English towns start to employ law enforcement officers.

1626: New York City Sheriff's Office founded.

1630s: Boston Night Watch founded.

1789: U.S. Marshals founded.

1791: Invention of guillotine.

1807: Richmond Police Department founded.

1844: New York City Police Department founded.

1854: Boston Police Department founded.

1855: Chicago Police Department founded.

1869: Los Angeles Police Department founded.

1886: U.S. Supreme Court determines that the federal government is responsible for interstate law enforcement in the case *Wabash v. Illinois.*

1905: First state police department founded in Pennsylvania.

1908: Federal Bureau of Investigation founded.

1910: Alice Stebbin Wells, first female police officer, sworn in as officer with the LAPD.

1964: Civil Rights Act of 1964, Title VII, forbids discrimination by employers on the basis of race, color, sex, religion, or national origin.

1991: Rodney King beaten by LAPD officers, leading to nationwide attention to police brutality.

1997: Abner Louima attacked by NYPD officers.

Chapter 2

State of the Industry

Law enforcement and public safety officers protect peoples' lives and property. They work as police officers, sheriffs' deputies, security guards, detectives, and special agents and inspectors. They patrol their jurisdictions, investigate suspicious activity, identify people who are breaking the law, and issue citations or warnings. Detectives and special agents may gather facts about criminal activities. All types of officers write reports of incidents, and many regularly appear in court to testify about cases in which they are involved.

Specific duties vary by law enforcement agency. City police have very different duties from officers who work for the Federal Bureau of Investigation (FBI). Game wardens may spend much of their time out of doors, while officers who handle traffic violations may spend their time on the road and university public safety officers spend their time patrolling college campuses.

Statistics on Employment, Wages, and Profits

What follows is a brief overview of the day-to-day terms of the law enforcement profession. Though many who enter this field are motivated by fine ideals of public service and the pursuit of justice, these more practical concerns are also essential to consider.

Hours and Working Conditions

Law enforcement work can be dangerous and require irregular hours. Officers regularly confront lawbreakers, who may be armed and willing to fight. They must be prepared to defend themselves and others from various types of assault. Body armor is a standard component of many law enforcement uniforms. Traffic policemen spend their days on the road, driving in traffic or stopping speeding vehicles, which puts them at risk of traffic accidents. Policemen are shot at by criminals, and they do sometimes die; anyone entering law enforcement must be aware of this risk. Notably, most assaults on law enforcement officers do not involve weapons more dangerous than hands and feet and are not deadly, but guns and knives do turn up. In 2008, 41 officers were killed in assaults with weapons, and about 60,000 were assaulted in the line of duty.

Salary and Wages

Very few law enforcement professionals get rich off their work, but most of them make a decent income. They also enjoy good job security and many of them get comfortable pensions after a relatively short time in their careers.

Most public safety and law enforcement officers receive more pay than their stated salaries because they are typically required to work many hours of overtime, which is paid at a higher hourly rate than regular work. Most officers receive the usual benefits such as medical and life insurance, paid vacation, and sick leave, and an additional allowance for uniforms. Police officers usually have very generous pension plans, and many retire at half pay after only 25 or 30 years of work. It is not unusual for retired officers to take on new jobs for the remaining years of their working lives.

According to the U.S. Bureau of Labor Statistics (BLS), the median annual salary for police and sheriffs patrol officers was $47,460 in 2006. The middle 50 percent of those officers earned between $35,600 and $59,880. The highest-paid officers earned over $72,000, while the lowest paid earned less than $27,310. The highest median earnings were for officers in state governments, who earned $52,540; the median for local government officers was $47,190, and for federal officers $43,510. The hourly mean wage for state officers in 2008 was $27.97; it was $25.23 for officers working for local governments. College and university public safety officers received the lowest pay, between $21 and $22 per hour.

Median earnings for police and detective supervisors was $69,310 in 2006. The highest-paid officers earned over $104,000, and the lowest-paid under $42,000. Supervisors who worked for the federal government earned the most, over $85,000; those who worked for state and local governments had median annual earnings of about $69,000.

The 2006 median annual earnings for detectives and criminal investigators was $58,260, though a few detectives earned over $92,000. Median annual earnings were highest in federal government positions, around $70,000, and closer to $50,000 for state and local government positions.

Federal employees who work in law enforcement receive special salary rates guaranteed by federal law. Deputy U.S. Marshals, for example are classified as GL-5 or GL-7 in the federal law enforcement pay scale; in 2008, those levels received salaries ranging from $36,658 to $46,969, depending on location. Anyone who applies for a job with a federal agency should ask their recruiter for information about salary rates and special law enforcement benefits packages. Federal special agents and inspectors, for example, are eligible for law enforcement availability pay (LEAP), to compensate for the large amount of overtime that they are required to work. This amounts to 25 percent of the agent's grade and step, a significant raise over base salary levels. High-ranking federal agents can make a very decent income, well over $100,000 a year, when LEAP pay is factored in.

Current and Future Trends in Law Enforcement

At the moment, law enforcement is a good field to be in. Jobs are plentiful and fairly secure. Law enforcement is somewhat recession-proof because people always expect protection from crime. As populations grow, law enforcement agencies must hire more officers to keep pace. On the other hand, most law enforcement departments are run by state and local governments, and are therefore at the mercy of government funding, so hiring varies from place to place based on local financial situations. Local law enforcement agencies—cities and counties—are a good place to look for jobs now.

According to the Bureau of Labor Statistics (BLS), about 861,000 people were employed as police officers and detectives in 2006. About four-fifths or 80 percent of them were employed by local

Fast Facts

Pay Grades

Federal employees are classified according to pay grades that are set by the General Schedule, or GS, pay scale, or the Law Enforcement Officer (LEO) pay scale, identified by the letters "GL". There are 15 grades in the GS scale. GS-1 is the lowest and GS-15 is the highest. Within each grade are 10 steps, each of which is paid slightly more than the step below it. The four highest steps of a grade are paid more than the lower steps of the next grade up. If you enter federal employment with a bachelor's degree you will probably start as a GS-5, though if you got very good grades you might start as a GS-7. A person with a master's degree may start at GS-9. Pay for each grade varies by city. In 2010, for example, starting salaries at the GS-5 level were $32,722 in Atlanta, $35,309 in New York City, and $37,073 in San Francisco. The LEO scale is similar, but is calibrated slightly differently. U.S. Marshals, for example, start as GL-5 or GL-7 and move up. Some people switch between pay scales, perhaps moving from a GL rate to a GS rate. Promotion possibilities are determined by job; some jobs expect employees to be promoted every year, while some cap promotion at a certain level.

governments, mainly cities and counties. The state police employed 11 percent and federal governmental agencies about 7 percent. The rest worked for contract security companies, educational services and universities, and rail transportation. Most city police work in cities with over 25,000 inhabitants, some of which have very large police forces. Thousands of small towns across the United States maintain very small police forces with fewer than 25 officers.

Job security is usually quite good and has been for many years. Layoffs are rare because most departments prefer to reduce their workforces through retirements. Officers who do lose their jobs due to budget cuts have little difficulty finding new employment with other law enforcement agencies because trained officers are in high demand. The public demands ever more security, so employment prospects for law enforcement and public safety officers are expected to be quite good. The BLS expects employment of police

Projected Occupational Data

Title	2006	Projected 2016
All Police and detectives	861,000	959,000
Supervisors/managers	93,000	102,000
Detectives and criminal investigators	106,000	125,000
Fish and game wardens	8,000	8,000
Police and sheriff's patrol officers	648,000	719,000
Transit and railroad police	5,600	5,900

Source: U.S. Bureau of Labor Statistics, http://www.bls.gov/oco/ocos160.htm

and detectives to grow 11 percent between 2006 and 2016, which is about average for all occupations.

Lots of Local Jobs

The greatest number of opportunities will be in local police departments; jobs in state and federal agencies will be tighter, and applicants for those positions will face more competition. Opportunities in local police departments should be excellent for qualified applicants. Departments will need to replace workers who retire or move to federal private sector jobs, and many departments will be growing as city populations get bigger. Job opportunities will vary in different locations and from year to year because government funding for law enforcement is not consistent.

The lowest competition for jobs will be in urban communities with low crime rates and in departments that offer the lowest salaries. Local and state departments will be looking for applicants with military experience or some college training in police science. Federal agencies will be looking for applicants with bachelor's degrees and several years of either military or law enforcement experience; experience in conducting investigations will be especially desirable.

Demand for Language Skills

Police forces are becoming increasingly international, reflecting the changing ethnic composition of the U.S. population. The New York

Police Department, for example, reported that it hired 5,593 officers between July 2006 and December 2009; of those, 1,042 were foreign born, and they came from 88 different countries. The Dominican Republic, Haiti, Pakistan, and Russia all supplied sizeable numbers of officers. This is partly the result of the department's explicit efforts to improve the diversity of its force. Officers who can speak foreign languages and understand different cultures are in particular demand.

Private Life and Working Conditions

Society's need for law enforcement never ends, and in fact is often greatest at night when many lawbreakers are active. Law enforcement officers may find themselves working at any hour of the day or night, and on any day of the year, including holidays. Most officers are scheduled to work 40 hours per week, but these 40 hours are composed of shifts that include every hour of the day, every day of the week. Policemen, detectives, and other law enforcement officers just starting out may have to work many night, weekend, and holiday shifts; as you gain seniority, you may get more control over your schedule. Long hours are common, especially during major investigations, and many law enforcement officers work a good deal of paid overtime.

Working conditions vary a great deal, but most officers do not spend their full working day behind a desk in an office. Patrol officers may spend most of their working hours in a squad car or on a motorcycle, driving around their jurisdictions. Some officers perform their patrol duties on bicycles, horses, or on foot. Game wardens and border patrol agents work out of doors, often in rough terrain. Federal agents may need to travel frequently, and may have to relocate their homes and families multiple times during their careers.

If you go into law enforcement or public safety, your job will not end when your shift does. Plan to carry your badge and maybe your weapon with you wherever you go. Most jurisdictions expect their police officers to be prepared to exercise their authority whenever necessary, whether or not they are on duty.

The Police Versus the Public

The police and the public sometimes have had a tense relationship. Law enforcement officers have the power to stop anyone they suspect of having committed a crime; just think about how you react when you notice a police car behind you. Police and other law enforcement agencies are often accused of abusing their authority through police brutality, racial profiling, intimidation, corruption, and other types of misconduct.

Law enforcement officers, for their part, often feel that the public does not support them in their mission to keep everyone safe. Officers regularly put their lives on the line and they find it very upsetting to have their actions second-guessed by outsiders. An officer who is confronted by a person he believes is violent wants to be able to take whatever action he feels necessary—even shooting the person—without having to face criticism and suggestions that he acted more violently than necessary.

Courtesy to the public, following department procedures, and being very precise in your work are the best ways to avoid accusations of misconduct. But do not expect to avoid this problem entirely. Accusations of police misconduct, some baseless and some very much based in reality, are a perennial aspect of life in law enforcement.

Fast
Facts

The Complexity of DNA Interpretation

Although many people believe that DNA evidence should make all criminal investigations clear-cut, the truth is more complicated. DNA data is often ambiguous and the quality of its interpretation depends on the skill and objectivity of analysts. Investigators type DNA by looking at 13 different sites, or loci, on a DNA strand. A small sample of DNA may not contain enough biological material to produce a complete profile; in this case, an analyst may not be able to tell if a mismatch in profiles is due to an inadequate sample or to true genetic differences. If a lab cannot make a complete profile of all 13 loci on a DNA strand, it may attempt to create a partial profile, which is inherently inaccurate because there is no way to tell what the complete profile would be. Sometimes DNA analysts know the facts of the case before they perform their analysis, which affects their interpretation of the DNA profiles. So DNA evidence can be helpful, but do not assume it is always conclusive.

How Dangerous is Law Enforcement?

How dangerous is law enforcement? The FBI compiles statistics on law enforcement officers killed and assaulted every year, which can give some idea of exactly what sort of risks officers face. In 2008, 41 officers were feloniously killed in the line of the duty, about half of them officers in city police departments. Of these officers, 37 were male. Their average age was 39 years, and their average length of law enforcement service was 10 years. Another 68 officers were killed accidentally, almost all of them in some sort of vehicular accident. For example, 13 officers were struck by vehicles while directing traffic or executing traffic stops. Nearly 60,000 officers were assaulted in the line of duty, and over a quarter of them sustained injuries. Disturbance calls account for 32 percent of these assaults. The vast majority of assaults were conducted with "personal weapons," which means hands or feet as opposed to firearms, knives, or other dangerous weapons. Clearly work in law enforcement is dangerous. Training and good equipment can help protect people who work in this field, but there will always be some risk of injury or death.

Important Technology

Law enforcement technology has improved tremendously in the past two decades. New methods of identifying people have made it easier to link suspects with crimes and to rule out innocent individuals.

Fingerprinting

The skin on the fingers is covered with hundreds of tiny ridges and valleys that form patterns—loops, whorls, and arches. These patterns are unique for every finger on every person and they never repeat. Even identical twins do not share fingerprints. Police departments began using fingerprints to identify criminal suspects in the late 1800s, and fingerprinting is widely used today as a means of identifying individuals. This is a complicated process. Basically, when a person touches an object, grease, sweat, and other substances on the ridges of his or her fingers leave marks on the object in the shape of the fingerprint. In practice, fingerprints are rarely perfect, and identifying them can be very difficult.

When a person is arrested, his or her fingerprints are taken at the police station or jail. The officer taking the fingerprints will cover the suspect's finger with ink and press them onto a card. Each finger is printed individually and rolled from one side of the fingernail to the other; these prints are called rolled impressions. The suspect then places all four fingers from each hand straight on the card simultaneously, followed by the same action with the thumbs; these flat impressions allow experts to double check the rolled impressions. The FBI maintains a database of fingerprints of over 50 million people, most of them criminal suspects. A police department can search the database to see if its new arrestees have ever been arrested before.

DNA Evidence

DNA is the portion of a gene that contains the genetic information used to develop an organism. All living things have DNA, from bacteria to humans. Every human's DNA profile is unique, which is what makes it so useful as a law enforcement tool. If a person leaves any physical substances at a crime scene—blood, semen, saliva—it is possible to analyze the DNA structure and compare it to other samples, such as a blood test taken from a suspect.

DNA testing can only be performed in cases where the criminal has left behind biological evidence, such as semen or blood. DNA tests produce three types of results: inclusion, exclusion, and inconclusive. If a DNA profile found at a crime scene matches the profile of a known person, that person is "included," or considered a possible source of the DNA sample; the rarer the profile within the population, the more likely the person is the source of the DNA. If a DNA profile from a crime scene does not match the DNA profile of a person, either suspect or victim, then the person is "excluded" as the source of the sample. If there is not enough information —if the sample is too small, if the DNA was of poor quality, or if it contains a mixture of DNA from several individuals—then the test may not be able to either include or exclude an individual as its donor. No DNA test can definitively prove a person's guilt; proving innocence is somewhat easier but still open to error.

DNA testing is not nearly as conclusive as many people believe. DNA testing presents numerous opportunities for technical mistakes. The most common type of testing, PCR-based testing, works by duplicating a strand of DNA millions of times, which makes it very vulnerable to contamination; if an officer at a crime scene simply sneezes, his or her own DNA can enter the sample and produce a misleading result. DNA can degrade quickly in hot or humid environments, especially if it is packed in plastic. Simply putting the wrong label a sample will produce an incorrect result because it can attach the sample to the wrong person, place, or time.

Although DNA is vulnerable to contamination and degradation, biological samples that have been properly collected, air dried, packed in paper, and properly labeled to ensure the chain of custody, can last for years, even stored at room temperature. This fact and the improvements in scientific methods in the past 15 years have allowed numerous men convicted of crimes in the past to be exonerated by post-conviction DNA testing.

DNA evidence can be used to exonerate people who have already been convicted of crimes, even after they have served many years of their sentences. As of early 2010, 250 people had been exonerated through post-conviction DNA testing. Several states have recently passed or proposed laws that would allow post-conviction review of biological evidence and the possible exoneration of convicts based on this evidence.

Forensic Science

Forensic science, or forensics, is the body of science concerned with answering questions about crimes, legal issues, and public issues. The word "forensic" comes from a Latin word meaning "related to the forum." The forum was the public place in a town in which politicians passed laws and citizens and judges held legal trials. Forensics technically refers to investigations done on matters of public interest, which is why the study of debate is also called forensics. In the law enforcement sphere, forensic science refers to objective investigations into crimes to be used for legal purposes, such as evidence in a criminal trial. Forensic scientists include doctors, lawyers, dentists, engineers, anthropologists, handwriting experts, and many other experts who investigate specific aspects of crimes. This is a growing field; scientific advances have made forensic science increasingly accurate and informative, and there will be a need for more trained experts to work in laboratories and analyze new types of evidence. There are many different types of forensic scientists:

➡ Criminalists identify and analyze physical evidence, such as blood, semen, DNA, hair, gasoline, footprints, and any other physical objects that can be left at a crime scene.

➡ Specialists in digital and multimedia sciences use cameras and computers to analyze and reconstruct crime scenes and identify suspects.

➡ Engineers help reconstruct the physical events of crimes and accidents.

➡ Forensic dentists use their expertise to identify unknown human remains and bite marks.

➡ Pathologists examine dead bodies to determine how they died.

➡ Physical anthropologists uncover and identify bodies discovered in the field; they try to determine how long ago the person died and if possible the mode of death.

➡ Psychiatrists and behavioral scientists assess mental stability, domestic issues, parental fitness, criminal motivations, and other psychiatric aspects of crimes.

➡ Document examiners analyze documents for handwriting, printer ink, signatures, additions and erasures, and similar clues.

➡ Toxicologists analyze chemical evidence to see if drugs, poisons, alcohol, or other substances played a role in a crime.

Weapons

Firearms are key weapons for most law enforcement officers. Many officers carry handguns in holsters as part of their uniforms. They may also have access to shotguns or rifles. Police often use pepper spray to subdue criminal suspects or for crowd control as a non-injurious alternative to the use of firearms. Pepper spray is a spray made from hot peppers, which contain a substance called capsaicin that makes people's skin and eyes burn. Pepper spray is made of capsaicin suspended in liquid and pressurized in an aerosol can. If sprayed on a person's face, it will make his eyes close immediately. He may also cough and have a hard time breathing. The effects can take hours to wear off completely. Water will not remove the spray, and rubbing the skin only makes it burn more.

Tasers are weapons that use electrical darts to subdue people. When a Taser is fired, two darts fly out and pierce the victim's skin. The darts stay connected to the device, which then sends an electrical charge through them. This causes the victim to lose control of his muscles. Some Tasers can also function as stunning devices when held directly against the victim's body. Tasers are popular in

law enforcement because they allow officers to subdue criminal suspects without getting too close and endangering themselves but also
without permanently injuring or killing the suspect with a firearm.
Tasers are not considered firearms because they do not use gun-
powder. Tasers are legal in most states in the United States for both
consumers (the general public) and law enforcement officers.

Major Players and Industry Forces

There are many forces that contribute to shaping and defining the
world of law enforcement. Knowing something of their backgrounds,
duties, and responsibilities is vital before beginning a job search.

State and Local Governments

Law enforcement organizations are usually run by governments.
Local governments such as cities and towns, counties, states, and
the federal government all have their own law enforcement organizations. Some governments have multiple law enforcement agencies; for example, New York City has city police; MTA police who
patrol subways and bus lines; and the Port Authority Police Department, which covers seaports, bridges, tunnels, and airports on the
New York–New Jersey border.

Because law enforcement organizations are government-run, they
can be at the mercy of voters and taxpayers. Pay, size of workforce,
and investment in new technology all depend on tax dollars. On
the other hand, law enforcement is considered a top priority in most
jurisdictions, so jobs are fairly secure, and the well-known dangers
of the job ensure that benefits are reasonably generous, especially in
the area of retirement.

The vast majority of law enforcement officers and staffers work
for cities and counties, serving as uniformed patrol officers for city
police and sheriffs' departments. Of the approximately 861,000 law
enforcement personnel working in 2006, about 648,000 of them were
patrol officers. Of those, about 548,000 worked for local governments.
About 60,000 worked for state governments, 11,000 for colleges and
universities, and another 11,000 for the federal government.

City Police
City police work for incorporated towns and cities throughout the
United States. Nearly every incorporated city has its own police

force that handles law enforcement matters within the city limits. City police employ both patrol officers to patrol the jurisdiction and respond to emergencies and detectives who investigate crimes that have already been committed. City police patrol assigned territories, or "beats," in automobiles, on foot, on motorcycles, or other modes of transport. They serve as a warning presence and are readily available to respond to crimes when they occur. They also direct traffic, serve legal processes of courts, testify in court, investigate accidents, and write reports on the incidents they have investigated.

City police are generally employees of the cities that run their departments. Most towns that grow to moderate size see the need for some sort of law enforcement organization and vote to create a police force. Municipal taxes cover police salaries and equipment.

Counties: Sheriffs and Sheriffs' Deputies

Sheriffs and sheriffs' deputies handle law enforcement within individual counties (or parishes in the case of Louisiana). The sheriff of a county is often an elected official. The actual law enforcement officers, however, are employees of the county. Officers who work for a sheriff are typically called sheriff's deputies or deputy sheriffs; terminology varies by county. The term "deputy" comes from the fact that the officers have been granted the same powers as the sheriff to uphold the law, or "deputized."

Sheriffs' departments generally perform law enforcement duties in unincorporated areas of their counties, leaving the city limits to city police. They guard county courthouses, run county law enforcement centers and jails, and conduct patrols, arrests, and investigations throughout their territories. They direct traffic, transport prisoners, serve notices and summons, seize property to satisfy judgments, and auction it off. They may support city police during busy times or special occasions.

State Police

Every state has its own state police that conduct law enforcement activities and criminal investigations within the state's borders. Every state has its own method of organizing state police. Some call their state police officers State Troopers. Some place their state police force within the state Department of Public Safety. Some states call their state police force the Highway Patrol, State Highway Patrol, or State Patrol.

Keeping in Touch

Developments in Telecommunications

Police have made use of telecommunications equipment ever since the invention of the telephone, but communications options today are much more complicated. A law enforcement office today will use radio communications equipment, teletype and computer systems linked to National Law Enforcement Telecommunications System (NLETS) or National Crime Information Center (NCIC), and various recording devices.

Law enforcement officers are allowed to set up secret surveillance systems if they get the appropriate permission. You cannot just set up a camera anywhere or wiretap anyone's telephone. You need to have a reasonable suspicion that a crime will occur and get a warrant from a judge granting you permission. Once you have permission, though, there is a great variety of equipment available for surveillance. Cameras, microphones, intelligent camera systems, built to be used indoors or outside and maybe to be supervised from surveillance vans—if you delight in working with electronic devices, this could be a great area for you.

The authority of state police usually extends to areas not specifically covered by city police or county sheriffs. This can include policing state and interstate highways, guarding state governors, protecting the state capitol, assisting local police officers in handling riots, labor disputes, or prison disturbances, providing security for large events such as football games, and providing high-level technological help to police forces in smaller jurisdictions. Some state police help train police officers for small towns that cannot devote their own resources to training. Some states allow state police to coordinate state-wide crime fighting efforts in complex cases.

Federal Law Enforcement

The highest-profile and most competitive law enforcement jobs are with the federal government. People typically enter these agencies

Everyone
Knows

Three Types of Firearms

Don't just call a gun a gun. There are three main types of firearms that every law enforcement officer should know. Handguns are firearms that are designed to be held in and shot with one hand, although many experts recommend using the other hand to support the weapon. Handguns include revolvers and pistols. Law enforcement officers often carry their handguns with them whenever they are on duty, wearing them in holsters on their hips or side. A shotgun is a firearm with a longer barrel and stock, designed to be held against the shoulder for firing. Shotguns shoot cartridges filled with small balls called shot. A shotgun's barrel is smooth. Because shot spreads when it is fired, it can cover wide area, making it easier to hit a target at close range. Shotguns also do not shoot very far or penetrate deeply, making them a useful firearm for shooting in close quarters. Rifles are also designed to be fired from the shoulder, but rifles are more often used for precise long-distance shooting. Rifles fire bullets. A rifle has spiral grooves inside its barrel, which make bullets spin as they leave the weapon, which helps its accuracy. A bullet shot from a rifle can fly a very long distance and, if the weapon is strong enough, can pass through walls or people and still retain some power. This makes rifles less than ideal for firing within city limits or buildings, but a rifle is ideal for distant shots that demand great precision. Law enforcement officers make use of all three types of firearm depending on the situation, and they do not call them guns. *Weapon* is the preferred generic term.

after several years experience in local law enforcement or the military, and usually with college degrees.

U.S. Marshals Service (USMS)

The U.S. Marshals Service is the oldest federal law enforcement agency, started by George Washington back in 1789. The USMS serves as the enforcement arm of the federal court system, and there are Marshals posted in all 94 federal judicial districts throughout the country. The agency employs about 3200 deputy marshals and criminal investigators. Their duties include protecting federal judges, apprehending federal fugitives and transporting federal prisoners, operating the Witness Security Program, investigating acts of terrorism and civil disturbances, and seizing property acquired illegally. In 2008, the U.S. Marshals arrested nearly 37,000 federal fugitive felons. The service houses about 58,000 detainees in jails and prisons throughout the nation; it has contracts to rent local jail space with about 1800 state and local governments. It manages about $1.7 billion worth of seized and forfeited property.

Federal Bureau of Investigation (FBI)
The Federal Bureau of Investigation is an agency of the United States Department of Justice charged with the investigation of crimes and law enforcement. Its mandate authorizes it to investigate all federal crimes that Congress has not assigned to another federal agency. Its mission includes investigating violations of federal criminal law, protecting the United States from terrorist activities, and assisting other federal, state, local, and international law enforcement agencies. In practice, the FBI's investigative work covers organized crime and drugs, financial crimes, counterterrorism, foreign intelligence, and civil rights. The FBI is headquartered in Washington, D.C., and works with officers in 56 field offices, about 400 satellite offices called resident agencies, four specialized field installations, and international liaison offices called legal attachés. As of 2009, the FBI employed nearly 33,000 people.

Department of Homeland Security (DHS)
The Department of Homeland Security exists to protect the United States from the many threats facing it, from terrorism to natural disasters. The DHS has five main areas of responsibility: guarding the country against terrorism, securing the borders, enforcing immigration laws, improving the nation's readiness for and recovery from disasters, and unifying itself as a department. DHS agents apprehend and deport illegal immigrants, fight drug violence within Mexico as a way of strengthening border security, conduct joint intelligence operations with other nations to combat international terrorism, and coordinate the government's response to events such as hurricanes, floods, and disease epidemics.

The DHS runs several agencies that specialize in various aspects of homeland security. These are:

1. Transportation Security Administration (TSA), which provides security for the nation's transportation systems, including airports and airlines.
2. U.S. Customs and Border Protection (CBP), which protects borders in an effort to keep out terrorists while still allowing free travel and trade for law-abiding individuals.
3. U.S. Citizenship and Immigration Services (CIS), which handles immigration and naturalization matters.
4. U.S. Immigration Customs Enforcement (ICE), an investigative agency that searches for vulnerabilities in national security and tries to eradicate them when it finds them.
5. U.S. Secret Service, a law enforcement agency that both protects the president and other high-ranking government officials and investigates counterfeiting, financial crimes, identity theft, and computer fraud.
6. Federal Emergency Management Agency (FEMA), which manages federal responses to natural disasters such as hurricanes.
7. U.S. Coast Guard, which patrols the nation's ports and waterways as well as other maritime regions.
8. Federal Law Enforcement Training Center (FLETC), an agency that provides training to law enforcement officers from all over the United States.
9. Domestic Nuclear Detection Office (DNDO), which looks for nuclear threats and coordinates responses to them.
10. National Cyber Security Division (NCSD), which protects cyberspace.

Bureau of Alcohol, Tobacco, Firearms, and Explosives (ATF)

The Bureau of Alcohol, Tobacco, Firearms, and Explosives, more commonly known as ATF, is a law enforcement agency within the U.S. Department of Justice dedicated to protecting communities from the trafficking of firearms, illegal transport of alcohol and tobacco, illegal use and storage of explosives, arson and bombings, criminal organizations, and violent crime in general. The ATF conducts investigations of crimes, regulates the firearms and explosives industries, and helps other law enforcement agencies in their handling of crimes involving alcohol, tobacco, firearms, and explosives.

Drug Enforcement Administration (DEA)
The Drug Enforcement Administration, or DEA, enforces laws regulating controlled substances, which include both legal and illegal
drugs. It was created by President Richard Nixon in 1973 as a first
step in starting the "war" on drugs. Its officers look for criminals
and gangs that are growing, manufacturing, or distributing illegal
drugs and bring them to court, seizing their assets in the process.
It also enforces the provisions of the Controlled Substances Act,
which regulates the manufacture, distribution, and dispensing of
legally produced controlled substances, such as prescription painkillers: only doctors can prescribe these drugs, and only licensed
pharmacies can legally dispense them, and prescriptions are only
valid for short periods of time. The DEA maintains a national drug
intelligence program that uses data collected by local, state, federal,
and foreign law enforcement organizations. Today the DEA employs
5235 Special Agents and operates 87 foreign offices in 63 countries.

Tribal Lands and Law Enforcement
Native American Indians living on tribal lands typically handle their
own law enforcement matters. There are over 200 Indian police
departments in the United States, keeping the peace in communities
ranging from the tiny Havasupai Tribe in the Grand Canyon, with a
population of about 600, to the 250,000-member Navajo Nation.

Most Indian police departments are organized under Public Law
93-638, the Indian Self-Determination and Education Assistance
Act of 1975. This law gives tribes the right to establish their own
government functions, including law enforcement organizations, by
contracting with the federal Bureau of Indian Affairs (BIA). Officers
and staff of these police departments are tribal employees. Tribes
also run their own judicial systems.

Indian police departments have fewer resources to work with
than police departments and must cover very large areas with few
officers. About 2,400 officers serve approximately 1.4 million Indians in the 56 million acres of tribal lands in the lower 48 states, less
than half the rate of coverage for small non-Indian communities.

Other Police Forces

There are numerous small, specialized law enforcement organizations throughout the country. These include:

1. College and University Public Safety departments, which handle matters of public safety on campuses and are not necessarily part of city or county law enforcement agencies.
2. The United States Postal Inspection Service, the law enforcement arm of the U.S. Postal Service, which fights mail fraud.
3. The Amtrak Police, which provides security for the Amtrak passenger train system; most of its officers work in the Northeast.
4. Public transit police forces, which protect public transportation systems such as the MTA in New York City.
5. The United States Park Police (USPP), which polices properties administered by the National Park Service and is the oldest uniformed federal law enforcement agency in the United States.

Issues of Law and Government Regulation

There are many bylaws, regulations, and standard procedures within the law enforcement world itself. Understanding some of these before entering the workforce can save you a tremendous amount of time and confusion.

Jurisdiction: Who Can Work Where

There are law enforcement agencies at nearly every conceivable governmental division and many nongovernmental ones. Cities, counties, states, and the federal government all have their own law enforcement agencies. Businesses and universities employ security guards and public safety officers; these may be employees of the business or university, or they may be employees of a company that provides contract security guards.

The interaction of all these different agencies can be very complicated. At the local level, counties and cities tend to divide up law enforcement duties between sheriffs and their deputies, who patrol the county, and city police, who patrol the city. The place where a crime occurs determines which law enforcement agency handles it; anything that happens inside city limits is technically the responsibility of the city police, whereas anything that happens in the county but outside city limits belongs to the sheriff's office. The precise details of this arrangement vary considerably from state to state and even from county to county within the same state. Some municipalities have merged their city and county law enforcement to avoid confusion. Las Vegas, for example, has a joint city-county police force run by an elected county sheriff.

The FBI only investigates crimes or possible crimes; it cannot prosecute them, relying instead on U.S. attorneys to decide which cases to prosecute and conducting the actual prosecutions.

Arrests and Warnings

When a law enforcement officer stops a person who is believed to have committed a crime, he may perform an arrest. The word "arrest" comes from a French word meaning "stop," and that is exactly what an arrest is: stopping a person from further action. If the alleged crime is serious, the police may handcuff the suspect, put him in a police vehicle, and bring him to the police station, jail, or law enforcement center.

Remember, you cannot stop anyone without probable cause. Probable cause means that you have seen and heard enough to have facts to support a reasonable belief that the person has been involved in some criminal activity. So, for example, if you see a car weaving erratically around the road, that would be probable cause for stopping the driver for a possible DUI.

An arrest is a serious matter because it deprives an individual of the right to act freely. For this reason, police are required to inform suspects that they have certain legal rights to protect them from incriminating themselves before they have a chance to talk to a lawyer. This information takes the form of a *Miranda warning*, named after a 1966 U.S. Supreme Court case. Different jurisdictions are allowed to make up their own

Everyone Knows

Union vs. Non-Union

Depending on your state, the police force may or may not be unionized. The International Union of Police Associations represents law enforcement officers, correctional officers, and support personnel throughout the United States and Canada. It is a member of the AFL-CIO. Unionized departments tend to have more job protection and more guaranteed pay raises than non-unionized ones. Check with your state to see if you will need to join the union to work in law enforcement.

INTERVIEW

Opportunities in the Industry

Jon Ripsky
Retired; Naperville, Illinois, Police Department;
Naperville Park District Chief of Police

How long have you worked in law enforcement? What jobs have you held?

I've worked in law enforcement in Naperville, Illinois, for over 40 years. Naperville is the fourth largest community in Illinois, located 30 miles west of Chicago. The police department is a nationally accredited agency, which delivers a high level of police service to a knowledgeable and demanding public. Over the years, I've served as a beat officer, a police sergeant, a police lieutenant, service division commander, and operations division commander. The services division was responsible for criminal investigation, records management and the 911 dispatch center. The operations division was responsible for criminal investigations, patrol service, traffic enforcement, juvenile services and animal control. The division had 116 employees. From 1991 through 2003 I worked as support service division commander, supervising 300 employees who handled accreditation, planning, training and research, record management, technical services, communications research, and the coordination of an annual budget of $22 million . I retired in 2003 and then came back in 2005 as chief of police for the Naperville Park District.

How did you get into law enforcement?

I was in the U.S. Navy when my father died. He had been a police officer in Naperville since the early 40s. When I was home for the funeral, the chief of police asked me if I would return to Naperville and

warnings, but they are all some variation of the form: "You have the right to remain silent. If you give up the right to remain silent, anything you say can and will be used against you in a court of law. You have the right to an attorney. If you desire an attorney and cannot afford one, an attorney will be obtained for you before police questioning." (See especially http://www.abanet.org/publiced/practical/criminal/miranda_rights.html.) Some states add a sentence asking the suspect if he or she understands those rights.

test for the job, so I did. I came onto the force as a beat officer in 1962, made police sergeant in 1972 and worked my way up to police lieutenant by 1975. I earned a B.A. in criminal justice in 1977 and an M.S. in management public service in 1980.

What sort of opportunities are there in the field of law enforcement and public safety? Do you see any areas growing more than others?
At this time most departments are cutting back; law enforcement and public safety are now being affected by the troubled economy. As the economy recovers, I believe that public safety will be one of the first industries to start rehiring. Local law enforcement will be the first to start rehiring.

What tips would you have for a person just starting out in a career in law enforcement?
The first thing I would advise anyone wanting to get into law enforcement is to have a minimum of a four-year degree, with the intent to do graduate work. The first thing I would tell a new hire is: Don't try to change the organization to be what you want it to be; you need to become a part of the organization. They should understand that it is important for them to become a part of the community they are serving; they are not to become an occupational force controlling the community. Integrity is everything in law enforcement.

What are the most important qualities a person needs to succeed in a law enforcement career?
A police officer needs to have a passion for helping people, doing what is right, honesty, the ability to think clearly when faced with trouble, [and the] willingness to change and to never stop learning. I also believe that local law enforcement with its contact with people where they live and work is the most satisfying career path in law enforcement, or, for that matter, the most satisfying of any career path at all.

Types of Crimes

Most jurisdictions divide crimes into more serious and less serious ones. As a law enforcement officer, you will need to know which is which. In the old common law system, most states used the term "felony" to refer to serious crimes such as assault, murder, rape, theft of large sums of money, and the like. The term "misdemeanor" referred to less serious crimes, such as possession of small amounts of controlled substances.

Today, many jurisdictions have either replaced these terms with terms such as "summary offense" or "petty crime" for misdemeanors and "indictable offense" to refer to felonies, which can only be tried after a grand jury has heard the charge and decided to issue a formal accusation of a crime. The punishments for serious crimes tend to be much harsher than those for petty crimes. Law enforcement officers have some discretion in determining what crimes people are accused of. Remember that a particular charge can have a big impact on a person's life.

Criminal Courts

When a person is arrested and accused of a crime, a day or so after the arrest he appears before a judge in a courtroom at an event called an arraignment, also known as an initial appearance or a bond hearing. You as the arresting officer may need to attend this hearing to testify as to what you have seen and why you arrested the person. At this event, the prosecutor and defense attorney each present a short version of the facts involved in the case. The judge decides whether or not to set bail, and if so, how much bail will be. If the judge sets bail, the accused can pay it and be released until the trial takes place, often some months hence. Sometimes the judge refuses to set bail, and the accused must remain in prison until trial.

Criminal suspects are often allowed to leave jail while they await trial. In many cases, the court will require the suspect to post bail, money that an accused deposits with the court as a pledge of his intention to return for trial. If he appears at trial he gets his money back, regardless of whether or not he is acquitted; if he does not appear on the appointed date, the court keeps the bail. Failing to return for trial is called "jumping bail" or "skipping bail," and is a crime in its own right. Bail is also called a bond, or a bail bond, because it represents a promise.

Trial Court

If you work in law enforcement, you will almost certainly have to appear in court from time to time to testify about your cases. Many people arrested of crimes plead guilty; in other words, they admit to having committed the crime in question and accept whatever punishment the criminal justice system gives them. In other cases, the trial court level is where most criminal cases are tried and concluded. Trial courts are called different names in different states—county court, district court, court of common pleas, or circuit court. (In New York, a trial court is called a "supreme court" for extra confusion.) Trial courts also include traffic court, family court, juvenile court, probate court, and many others. At the federal level, trial courts are called "district courts."

At trial, the party bringing the lawsuit is called the "plaintiff." The party defending itself is called the "defendant." In criminal cases, the government brings a lawsuit against a person accused of a crime, who is called a defendant. In civil cases, both plaintiff and defendant are private citizens. When you read the name of a court case, the first party listed is the plaintiff; the one after the "v." is the defendant. In other words, a case name will be written "*Plaintiff v. Defendant.*"

The trial court determines questions of fact and questions of law. Questions of fact concern what exactly happened in the case before the court. Who did what to whom? When did all of it happen? The lawyers presenting the case use various types of evidence to establish the facts that they want the judge or jury to believe. They will ask questions of the parties and witnesses, show exhibits, and make speeches in which they try to convince the judge or jury that their side is correct. The arresting officer is often a key witness in a criminal trial. If you are called to the stand, you will have to swear to tell the truth and then describe exactly what happened when you arrested the defendant. The defending attorney will also ask you questions and possibly try to catch you in some mistake. Do not let that throw off your concentration. Just tell the truth and stay calm.

At trial, the "fact finder" decides which facts are relevant and determines whether the plaintiff has met the burden of proof. The fact finder can be either a judge or a jury. If a judge makes the decision, the trial is called a bench trial. If a jury decides, it is called a jury trial. The jury's final decision is called a verdict. The judgment is the amount of money or other remedy awarded to the prevailing party by the court.

Appellate Court (Court of Appeals)

If a party to a lawsuit is unhappy with the trial court's decision, he or she can appeal to a higher court. These higher courts are known as appellate courts, or courts of appeals. Witnesses, including law enforcement officers, do not testify before appeals courts. An appeals court considers only questions of law, such as whether the trial court applied the law correctly to the facts. The appeals court uses the facts that were established at trial, as set forth in the record of the trial. That means that an appeal does not involve exhibits of evidence or cross-examination of witnesses. Instead, the lawyers for the parties present written briefs and oral arguments in which they try to convince the judges that the trial court applied the law improperly, made a procedural error, reached a verdict not supported by the weight of the evidence, or committed another legal error.

The party who brings the appeal is called the "appellant" and the other party the "respondent." At the state level, there are many different appeals structures. Some states have an intermediate appeals court, for first appeals. If a party does not like the decision of the first appeals court, it can appeal to the state's highest court. The highest court is called "supreme court" in most states, but not all of them.

The decisions that come out of appeals are very important. After a judge hears a case, he or she writes an explanation of his or her decision. This document examines the statutory law and case law that applies to the matter, consider the decisions past courts have made in similar situations, and explain the judge's reasoning in arriving at a decision. From then on, lawyers and other judges will read this decision and use it in formulating their legal arguments. The decision will become a "precedent" and will effectively function as established law.

Supreme Court

Cases involving law enforcement officers occasionally make it all the way to the United States Supreme Court, which passes down decisions that become the law of the land. The Miranda warning, for example, came out of the 1968 Supreme Court case *Miranda v. Arizona*. In this case, a suspect who had been arrested for one crime confessed to having committed a different, earlier crime while he was being interrogated by the police. The Court ruled that this was self-incrimination in violation of the Fifth Amendment of the U.S. Constitution, and that the police should have informed him that he had a right to an attorney and that he did not have to say anything at all to police questioning. In *Maryland v. Wilson* (1997), a state trooper stopped a car, noticed that the passenger was nervous, and ordered him out of the car. The passenger dropped a bag of cocaine and the officer arrested him for possession with intent to distribute. The trial court and appeals court ruled that this constituted an unreasonable search and seizure, but the Supreme Court reversed, holding that officers are allowed to order passengers to get out of the car during a routine traffic stop. You never know when you may be involved in an arrest that will change national law!

Correctional Systems

Correctional institutions throughout the nation employ a large number of officers. Even if you do not work at a correctional institution, if you work in law enforcement you will certainly have contact with prisons, jails, penitentiaries, and local law enforcement centers.

The type of correctional institution used to house an individual depends on the crime committed and the stage of the conviction process. When a law enforcement officer arrests a suspect, he or she often delivers the individual to the local jail or law enforcement center. Jails are typically used for short-term detention of people who have been arrested for crimes but not yet convicted of them. Officers who receive suspects at jails may fingerprint them, place them in cells, help them contact friends, relatives, and attorneys, and ask them questions about the crimes they are suspected of having committed.

Suspects usually do not enter prison until after they have been tried and convicted of a crime. Prisons and penitentiaries are facilities that house convicted criminals for the duration of their sentences. Suspects may also be held in prison while awaiting trial or if they are denied bail or cannot afford it.

Fast Facts

Pleading the Fifth

"Pleading the Fifth" means refusing to answer police questions. This is a big deal because anything a suspect says to police questioning could potentially be used against him or her in court. Statements to the police can have the weight of "testimonial evidence," factual statements that can be used to prove the person's guilt. The Fifth Amendment of the U.S. Constitution states that no person "shall be compelled in any criminal case to be a witness against himself." That means anyone who is arrested is allowed to keep his mouth shut when questioned about his alleged crime.

There are many different types of prison. Which prison a convict enters depends on the type of crime he or she committed. People who did not commit violent crimes and who are not deemed very dangerous may be sent to minimum-security facilities. They are given a fair amount of freedom to roam the grounds and socialize with other inmates. Maximum-security prisons are for inmates who are considered very dangerous to other people, including prison staff and other inmates. These facilities have a great deal of supervision and numerous security measures to keep inmates inside and out of trouble. The most dangerous inmates may end up in supermax prisons, where they are kept in solitary confinement and only let out

Everyone
Knows

The Role of the Bondsman

Bail bondsmen and bounty hunters are important players in the law enforcement world. When an accused and his family cannot afford to pay bail themselves, they may choose to borrow the money from a bail bondsman. For example, if a person's bail is set at $30,000, the bondsman will post the total amount with the court in exchange for $3,000 from the accused, paid up front. They usually demand some collateral in addition to their percentage fee such as a life insurance policy, jewelry, or any other valuable item. The bondsman will return the collateral when he gets his bail money back from the court. If the accused jumps bail, the bondsman keeps the collateral.

Bondsmen prefer to have a member of the accused person's family co-sign the loan and promise to pay back the full amount of bail if the bondsman must forfeit it. When the accused returns for trial, the court pays back the bail and the bondsman makes his profit. If the accused fails to turn up, the bondsman forfeits the entire amount of bail. If an accused runs away before court, the bondsman may employ a bounty hunter to catch him and bring him back to the police. Each state has its own laws regulating bail bondsmen and bounty hunters; bail bonding and bounty hunting are illegal in some states.

for brief periods every day. Maximum security prisons may include supermax units for the absolute worst inmates; inmates in this section may each live in individual cells under 24-hour supervision.

When an inmate has completed a sentence, he or she typically spends some time on parole, a period of supervised freedom. During parole, the former inmate is free to live where he wants to, move about as he wishes, and work where he likes within limits imposed by the judge or correctional system. These limits may include regular meetings with a parole officer, getting a job, and not getting arrested again. Parole boards may decide to parole inmates before the ends of their sentences if they have behaved themselves well in prison; this is considered a good way of rehabilitating inmates who appear to have reformed.

Organized Crime

Organized crime has been a problem for U.S. law enforcement for years. The best-known organized crime groups are the Italian organizations collectively known as the Mafia. The Mafia evolved as a form of vigilante justice in Italy, as poor locals fought back against oppressive landowners. When large numbers of Italians immigrated to the United States in the late nineteenth and early twentieth centuries, they brought the Mafia with them. The first major Mafia incident took place in New Orleans in 1890, when Sicilians were suspected of murdering the city police superintendent. Over the twentieth century Mafia groups grew rich and influential by working in a number of illegal or shady areas: gambling, prostitution, construction, drug trafficking, labor racketeering, loan sharking, money laundering, and bootlegging have all been sources of profit for organized crime groups.

Today the FBI keeps track of several Mafia groups, including the Sicilian Mafia, the Camorra or Neapolitan Mafia, and the Calabrian Mafia. All of these groups maintain ties with their brothers in Italy, where organized crime has thrived since the mid-1900s. Organized crime is not all Italian, though. The FBI is also keeping tabs on a number of Eurasian and Asian crime groups that operate internationally. Their activities include prostitution, gambling, drug trafficking, insurance and credit card fraud, theft, and human trafficking. Federal law enforcement agents combat these newer organizations with the techniques that they have honed over decades of Mafia work: undercover operations, electronic surveillance, informants, and the enterprise theory of investigation, which tries to implicate entire groups in criminal acts, not just individuals.

Juveniles and Crime

Juvenile justice is a unique category of criminal justice. About 6 percent of young people under the age of 18 are arrested every year; about 6 percent of those arrested are arrested for violent crimes and the rest for non-violent offenses. Gang activity is perhaps the worst source of juvenile crime. Gangs have guns and drugs, and most juvenile murders are linked to gangs.

Legally, children under the age of 18 are not held completely responsible for their actions; for instance, contracts made by minors are usually not legally binding. Many people believe that most children and teenagers can be reformed, no matter how bad their behavior. Incarcerating children with adults is known to be very bad for the children, who are very likely to be abused in prison. There is continuing debate about how to handle juvenile offenders. Some people want them to be tried and sentenced as adults. Others point to evidence that this type of treatment is the best way to create life-long criminals and that educational programs specifically designed for juveniles are much more effective at teaching accountability and life skills.

Law enforcement departments usually keep juveniles separate from adult offenders. Some officers specialize in juvenile crime. The means of persecuting, trying, and reforming juvenile offenders is constantly evolving. It will continue to necessitate the efforts of devoted law enforcement officials nationwide.

Chapter 3

On the Job

Most law enforcement organizations are hierarchically organized. The line of promotion may look like this:

1. Cadet/probationary officer: A trainee or a rookie officer who works under the supervision of a more senior officer.
2. Officer: A fully trained patrolman who can operate independently. There may be several levels of officer, with increasing pay and responsibility dependent on seniority and track record.
3. Sergeant: A fully trained officer in charge of a group of officers.
4. Lieutenant: A fully trained sergeant in charge of several sergeants and their officers, and also entrusted with helping the Captain with administrative duties.
5. Captain: A fully trained lieutenant in charge of an entire precinct or division.
6. Chief: A fully trained captain in charge of an entire department.
7. Commissioner: The most senior official in an agency.

Depending on the organization, ranks may be divided into multiple levels or grades with increasing levels of responsibility and pay. Advancement to the higher levels may require an officer to earn a college degree and pass an examination. Some of the highest ranks are political appointments.

Many law enforcement organizations have officers who work in specialized areas that do not fit so precisely into this rank structure. For example, police detectives may technically outrank junior officers but not be on a direct trajectory to lieutenant or captain. Each organization has its own structure. If you go into law enforcement, it should not be hard to identify lines of promotion and seniority within your organization.

State and Local Law Enforcement Positions

The following positions are found at the state and local levels. Though law enforcement officials in these positions focus on issues of local concern, they may collaborate with national agencies for certain cases. Experience at this level is highly recommended if you wish to seek a federal position.

Chief Deputy

In many counties, the chief deputy is the officer who actually runs the daily law enforcement operations of the sheriff's office. A chief deputy is usually appointed, as opposed to the sheriff, who is elected. The chief deputy serves as the operations manager for the whole office, including supervising all the different sections within the office such as administration, criminal investigations, and detention. The chief deputy's office handles all administration, including hiring, firing, and other personnel issues; budgets, logistics, development of new programs and coordination of existing ones; and anything else involved in managing a large law enforcement operation.

Chief of Police/Commissioner

The chief of police is the highest ranking officer in a police department. He or she is in charge of the entire department's planning, administration, and operation. This involves attending many meetings, testifying before city councils and legislatures about the activities and needs of the police department, speaking to the media, and making presentations to various community groups about law enforcement. The chief of police also presents awards to valorous officers and disciplines officers who have committed infractions. The chief of police is usually a politically appointed position with a set term; often the mayor appoints the chief. In large cities, the chief of police is usually required to have a four-year college degree and many years experience on the police force. Requirements may be less stringent in small towns, where the chief of police is sometimes the only paid member of the police force.

Dispatcher

Dispatchers are the people who handle communication among law enforcement officers and their departments. Dispatchers receive incoming calls reporting crimes and other incidents and relay that information to officers who can respond. Some dispatchers work for the 911 number, receiving all types of emergency calls and then deciding which force to call out—firefighters, paramedics, or law enforcement. Police and sheriffs' departments employ dispatchers to handle all their communication. This is a good job for someone who can handle a fast-paced work environment and who can quickly decide what needs to be done to solve a problem. A dispatcher listening to an emotionally distraught caller must be able to identify the nature of a problem, its location, its seriousness, and the best possible response to it in a very short amount of time. Making mistakes can have serious consequences because emergency help might not arrive in time. At busy times, the calls may not stop coming for an entire shift.

Domestic Violence Officer

A domestic violence officer (who can be either a civilian or a sworn officer) handles cases of domestic violence. A number of complaints to police and sheriffs' departments involve domestic violence, such as husbands attacking wives. These complaints are often difficult to handle because the victims and their attackers often live in the same home, may share children, and the parties involved are often not sure whether a crime has occurred. Domestic violence officers are trained to provide crisis counseling to victims, help with crime scene investigations by photographing victims' injuries, taking statements from victims and witnesses, investigating the history behind incidents, referring victims to agencies that can help them and advising them on the criminal justice system, maintaining files on domestic violence cases, and following up on cases. Law enforcement departments typically want domestic violence officers to have a bachelor's degree in psychology, social services, or a similar field, or several

Everyone Knows

Sworn Officers and Civilians

Most people who work in law enforcement are sworn officers. This means that when they became officers they swore an oath to uphold the Constitution of the United States and the laws of the nation and their state and city or county. Sworn officers are authorized to carry firearms and arrest people. Though descriptions vary by state, the primary responsibility of sworn officers is to enforce the laws of the jurisdiction and to detect and prevent crimes. Law enforcement agencies also employ a number of civilians, who are not authorized to make arrests. These civilians are ordinary employees, who come to work, are paid a wage or salary, but have not sworn any oath promising to behave in a certain way. Depending on the office, scientists, administrative workers, forensics specialists, social workers, and other employees may be civilians.

years experience working in social services. Domestic violence officers need good communication skills and should be prepared to work nights and weekends.

Fish and Game Warden

Do you enjoy getting out in the woods or out on the water? You may like putting your wilderness expertise to use as a fish and game warden. In this job, you would be part law enforcement officer and part wildlife biologist. Fish and game wardens patrol assigned territories to look for violations of hunting and fishing laws, including making sure that hunters and fishermen carry the proper license and that they have not bagged too many animals or the wrong kind of animal entirely. Wardens also conduct wildlife surveys to assess the health of populations of wild animals. They may also investigate complaints of property damage by wild animals, capture or kill animals that are causing problems, and visit schools and community centers to teach people about hunting and fishing laws. Most fish and game wardens are employed by state governments.

Highway Patrol Officer/State Police Officer/ State Trooper

Do you like driving? You had better like it if you intend to work for the state police. Though organizations vary by state, state police agencies have jurisdiction over most of the major highways in the state, including interstate highways, state highways, freeways, and all roads in unincorporated areas (i.e., roads that are not within city limits). Highway patrol officers spend much of their time patrolling the highways, stopping speeders, looking for vehicles that belong to known criminal suspects, and responding to calls of accidents. State police usually have full law enforcement powers as well and can respond to any crime or enforce laws anywhere within their states of jurisdiction.

Juvenile Officer

Do you like working with kids? Juvenile officers handle all aspects of law enforcement that involve young people. Kids commit a wide variety of crimes, from theft to rape to murder on occasion. For the most part, though, the criminal justice system assumes that children and teenagers are not yet hardened criminals, and that they can be encouraged to reform themselves before they head irreparably down the path of crime. The work juvenile officers do reflects this hope. Juvenile officers handle the paperwork and filing that accompany juvenile arrests, and communicate with state departments of children or family services. They may also mentor young people who need role models, sponsor community activity programs intended to keep kids off the streets, return runaways to their parents, work with faith-based and community initiatives, and help former young offenders find jobs or get back into school. This is a good position for someone with an optimistic personality.

K9 Officer

Do you love dogs? If you get a job as a K9 officer, you can spend all day every day in the company of your best canine friend. "K9" is an acronym for the word *canine*, which means "dog." K9 officers work with dogs that have been specially trained to do law enforcement jobs. Dogs are very useful to law enforcement because they have very sensitive noses and are fast, strong, and good at bringing down prey. German shepherds are the best-known police dogs, but law enforcement officers also use other breeds such as bloodhounds for tracking people and beagles for sniffing out explosives and drugs. K9 cops and their dog partners typically do their training together. The dog may learn to sniff for drugs, dead bodies, bombs, or other devices, how to chase down and subdue people (without killing them), and how to behave when not actively performing duty. As a K9 officer, you would learn how to do patrols with your dog, how to handle a leash and a sidearm simultaneously, how to send your dog off to attack, and how to call him off once his job is done. Police dogs and their officers often form very close bonds; the dogs live with their officer-partners and become part of their families. To become a K9 officer, you will need to spend at least a year or two on the force as a patrolman, and then undergo rigorous and time-consuming training with your dog partner. You will also need to be prepared to spend the next several years of your life caring for that dog every single day and night—great news for a dog-lover!

Narcotics Officer

A narcotics officer, often called a "narc," is a police officer who investigates crimes involving illegal drugs. Narcotics officers often work undercover, disguising themselves as members of drug gangs in order to discover who is selling drugs and where they are getting them. In order to become a narcotics officer, you will first need to become a police officer by attending the police academy. Many departments require narcotics officers to undergo specialized training in their field in order to make them more effective and less likely to be spotted and perhaps killed by their subjects. Most states now have narcotic officer associations that provide specialized drug enforcement training for officers.

Plainclothes Police Officer

A plainclothes police officer wears civilian street clothes instead of a police uniform while going about his or her duties. This makes it easy for the officer to blend in with ordinary people instead of standing out as a police officer. An officer who wears plainclothes may not be working undercover, but simply wearing civilian clothes. Plainclothes officers usually work under their own names, carry ordinary police equipment, and readily identify themselves when making arrests.

Police Captain/Major

A police captain or major supervises an entire police station. (Different cities have different ranking systems, and a captain in some cities is the same as a major in others. Some cities also have higher-ranking officers such as colonels, but the job description is more or less the same, just with greater and greater responsibility.) A captain inspects all officers and equipment to make sure that all gear and individuals comply with regulations, makes sure officers and detectives are following department policies, oversees crime investigations, and generally ensures that the department functions as it should. A good captain delegates much of this work to lieutenants, sergeants, and higher-ranking police officers, but always ensures that they are doing their jobs correctly. Captains must spend a lot of their time communicating with municipal leaders and citizens' groups to maintain good relations with the general public. Captains also have many administrative duties such as reviewing correspondence, approving budget requests, teaching at the police academy, and interviewing and hiring applicants for the police force.

Police Detective

Many police departments employ detectives, who are officers with specialized training in criminal investigation. To become a detective, an officer must usually first complete the probationary period with satisfactory results and be chosen for the detective ranks. Much of the training is on the job. Police departments may rank their detectives, such as Detectives I, II, and III. Detectives at all ranks visit crime scenes, conduct investigations, perform surveillance, apprehend suspects, administer polygraphs, prepare reports, and testify in court. They may need to travel to other cities or even overseas to investigate crimes. Higher-ranking detectives are responsible for the training and supervision of novices. The highest-ranking detectives lead the investigations of the most important high-profile crimes, assigning officers to tasks, reviewing reports prepared by their subordinates, coordinating investigations with civilian organizations, and handling administrative details. This is a good rank to aim for if you enjoy handling "big picture" problems and do not mind spending a lot of your time at a desk. Many detectives are assigned to specialized departments. Large cities may have detectives who specialize in fields such as homicide, fraud, auto theft, juvenile crime, narcotics, child abuse, or sex activities. Smaller city detectives may not be quite so specialized.

Police Lieutenant

A police lieutenant supervises several sergeants and their squads, including detectives and police officers. The lieutenant is the captain's direct assistant, and serves as commanding officer of the division when the captain is not available. Lieutenants may be assigned large geographic areas for which they must oversee all crime-fighting activity. They must make sure that the correct number of officers is sent out to visit crime scenes or to patrol an area based on its history of criminal activity. They also review all reports and order follow-up when necessary, respond to the scenes of major crimes such as shootings that involve officers, and inform the police captain of all important information. Lieutenants must also perform activities such as reviewing correspondence, interviewing suspects and witnesses, teaching at the police academy, and speaking to community groups about police activities. Some lieutenants are assigned to specialized divisions while others handle general police work. Large departments may have multiple ranks of lieutenant. Lieutenant positions are difficult to land. They tend to go to officers with years of experience, high test scores, excellent performance reviews, qualifications such as four-year college degrees, and proven leadership skills.

Police Officer/Patrolman/Patrol Officer

The vast majority of sworn officers in a police force are called police officers or patrolmen. Police officers do the daily work of law enforcement, responding to reports of crimes or accidents, interviewing witnesses, directing traffic, booking suspects, and all the other duties that are involved in law enforcement. A police officer may walk a beat on foot, drive around in a patrol car, ride bicycles or motorcycles, or cover his or her territory on horseback. Some officers fly helicopters or work with air support divisions. Some specialize in areas such as narcotics, juvenile crime, traffic, or domestic violence.

Police Officer I/Probationary Officer

A Police officer I is actually a probationary officer. New officers who have recently completed the police academy hold this rank until they have completed their probationary periods and proven that they can handle all their duties. A police officer I will be assigned to a geographic patrol division under the supervision of a higher-

Best Practice

Pay Grades

Most police departments have several grades of police officer classified based on seniority and pay. Every department has its own system of organization, so consult with your city police for the details of its rank structure. Most departments, however, have a clear hierarchy of officers, starting with probationary officers and going up to high-ranking administrators. Large cities use structures similar to the one outlined here, though terminology varies from department to department.

ranking officer. Probationary officers perform all basic policing duties, including going to the sites of crimes or accidents, writing crime reports, monitoring suspicious activities, booking suspects, talking to community members as part of the community policing effort, preparing daily reports, and many other activities.

Some new officers are assigned to specialized divisions, such as juvenile narcotics, in which they may be required to patrol local schools for narcotics activities, or traffic enforcement, in which they search for drunk drivers, catch speeding drivers, assist at accidents, and appear in traffic court. In order to move up from this probationary level, an officer must serve for a specific period of time and receive satisfactory evaluations and test scores. The whole point of the probationary period is to give rookie officers a chance to gain experience while under the supervision of senior officers; once the department is satisfied that their rookies have become experienced officers who can handle work on their own, they move on up.

Police Officer II

After completing a probationary period, which may take from one to three years, officers continue to perform basic duties but are given much more responsibility and authority over junior officers. This is the level at which officers begin specialized training to become detectives, SWAT team members, K9 specialists, vice investigators, and many other positions. Large city police departments have many specialties and subdivisions, so there are many opportunities available to officers whose careers are going well. Officers at this rank may put some time into extra education, such the study of criminal justice at a community college, which can help them get promotions.

Police Officer III

After several years of experience and with a track record of success, a police officer may be promoted to the highest rank of police officers. At the police officer III level, officers take on many positions of responsibility. They lead groups of officers, plan investigations and operations, and handle the training of new recruits. Many departments like to assign probationary officers to the supervision of an officer with a good deal of experience and leadership ability. Advanced level officers may also take on positions that put them in contact with the public and the news media, such as media relations coordinator or legislative officer. Some officers finish their careers at this level. Others use their promotions as a way to move into other ranks, such as detective, sergeant, or chief of police.

Police Sergeant

A police sergeant supervises groups of officers on different shifts or geographical areas. Large departments may have multiple ranks of sergeant, such as Sergeants I, II, and III; the higher-ranking sergeants handle the most complex work. Sergeants are in charge of making sure that the work of patrol officers goes smoothly. They plan car assignments, inspect officers and their equipment, take radio calls and dispatch officers to the scenes of crimes or accidents, arrange for the assignment and training of probationary officers, review the reports that officers bring in, and any other similar tasks related to on-the-ground organization of police squads.

Sergeants often specialize in particular areas, such as narcotics, homicide, vice, or juvenile affairs. Sergeants with experience as K9 or mounted officers may use their expertise running those departments. The life of a sergeant is not all deskwork, though; they do go out on patrol and may even get to do things such as fly helicopters to perform air surveillance. The qualifications needed to become a sergeant vary by department and specialty, but in all cases a sergeant will need a good track record of skilled work and knowledge of police procedures.

Sheriff

A sheriff is usually the highest law enforcement officer in a county. The sheriff's police equivalent might be the chief of police of a city. Depending on the county, the sheriff is either elected or appointed. A sheriff may be in charge of the county jail. Some sheriffs also serve as coroners, in charge of recovering dead bodies and issuing death certificates. In some counties the sheriff is the official tax collector. The bulk of a sheriff's law enforcement duties are actually performed by a number of officers known as deputies, who are deputized to perform the sheriff's responsibilities. These officers function as county police officers.

Sheriff's Deputy

Sheriffs' deputies or sheriffs' patrol officers do the same jobs as city police but in a county, not a city. The term *deputy* comes from that fact that law enforcement officers working for a county are authorized, or deputized, to perform the sheriff's duties. As a sheriff's deputy you may patrol an area on foot or in a car, apprehend and arrest people suspected of crimes, investigate crimes, direct traffic, stop drivers and issue citations, investigate traffic accidents, serve process, or any number of other law enforcement duties. Some sheriffs' deputies specialize in vice, narcotics, or other areas. They may spend time undercover, infiltrating groups of criminals such as crystal methamphetamine dealers. Sheriffs' deputies may also work in tax collection, emergency disaster relief, or county civil defense.

Social Worker

A social worker works with people to help them cope with the difficulties they face in their lives. In law enforcement, social workers might help people with issues around substance abuse, domestic violence, child abuse, truancy, homelessness, poverty, mental illness, and all the other social ills that surround crimes. Social workers can help ease convicts back into society after they have spent time in prison. Many states are currently investing in programs that use social workers to help substance abusers in treatment programs instead of sending them to prison. Most social workers have at least a bachelor's degree, though many have master's degrees. Every state has licensing requirements, which might be necessary to get a job. This is a good job for someone who likes to help others, but do realize that if you go into social work you will be facing complex and often dire problems on a regular basis. You will need to be sensitive, responsible, and emotionally mature.

SWAT Team

Do you dream about being in the military's special forces? Better yet, do you have experience as an Army Ranger, a Navy SEAL, or a Green Beret? You might find job satisfaction working on a police SWAT Team. SWAT stands for "Special Weapons and Tactics." SWAT teams are specially trained and equipped to handle violent crises— terrorist attacks, hostage situations, riots, bombings, and other unusually dangerous situations. SWAT team members are given powerful weapons, body armor, and advanced training in tactics and teamwork. They learn how to stay calm under pressure and to work with their team members to achieve objectives. They may also practice specialized skills such as rappelling, entering buildings, handling explosives, and close-quarters self-defense. Life as a SWAT officer is not all hostage recoveries and bomb defusing, though; extraordinary crises do not come up all that often, so most SWAT-qualified officers work as ordinary police officers most of the time. SWAT forces are selective. To become a member, you will need some experience in a police department, and then will have to pass several physical and written tests to prove that you are physically and intellectually capable of handling the challenges of SWAT operations. This is a good position to aim for if your goal is higher rank in the police force; SWAT officers are often considered good candidates for promotion.

Undercover Agent

An undercover agent is a police officer, maybe a detective, who pretends to be someone else in order to gather information about criminal operations. They dress in the style of their target suspects; for example, an undercover agent who is investigating a ring of drug dealers will dress and act like the drug dealers. They often befriend their subjects in order to win their trust and gain access to their activities. Undercover agents often set their own hours and decide for themselves where to go and what to work on. This might be a good field for you if you are a good actor and like to work independently. You will need a high tolerance for stress; undercover agents are often exposed to dangerous and uncomfortable situations, and can never reveal their true identities while they are working.

Vice Police

Vice police concentrate on stopping vice—gambling; illegal sales of alcohol, drug and weapon violations; prostitution; and unlawful pornography. Vice officers work in teams or individually. They may work undercover, disguising themselves to infiltrate gangs of criminals. The crimes that fall under the vice heading are often the work of well-organized groups including the Mafia, so if you go into this field you may be in the midst of the organized crime world. If you want to become a vice officer, you will need to have some experience as a regular uniformed officer, typically one to three years. Some police departments recruit rookie officers for this area based on their appearance, language skills, or probable ability to thrive in the stressful environment of undercover work. Learning a foreign language can enhance your chances of getting this type of job. Doing well on departmental exams and getting good evaluations in your early work will also help. It can also help if you are willing to work somewhere other than your hometown. Anonymity is very important in this field, so departments often try to use officers who are not known to local criminals. The pay in this area can be good, up to $100,000 a year for top earners. Most of these jobs are in city police departments and competition is stiff for positions with federal and state agencies.

Victim Advocate

Many county courthouses, police departments, and district attorney's offices employ victim advocates to help the victims of crimes, particularly victims of sexual assault or domestic violence. If you go into this field, you may help victims give statements, fill out forms, and file for injunctions. You may go with victims to medical appointments and court appearances. You will need to keep up with the laws on victims' rights. Victim advocates also do community outreach to help people learn how to avoid domestic violence. You may spend much of your time in an office, or you may travel around to visit victims in their homes and to handle presentations at community centers. Victim advocates generally have an associate's or bachelor's degree in social work, counseling, or a similar field. Language abilities are especially useful in this field, as is a genuine desire to help people.

Federal Law Enforcement Positions

The positions outlined here are the domain of the federal government. The officers and agents in these positions may be called to work with state and local agencies as well as those at the international level.

Bureau of Alcohol, Tobacco, and Firearms (ATF) Special Agent

The Bureau of Alcohol, Tobacco, and Firearms investigates violations of federal laws involving alcohol, tobacco, firearms, explosives, and arson. As an ATF special agent, you would perform surveillance, interview suspects and witnesses, arrest criminal suspects, issue search warrants and search premises for evidence of crimes, prepare case reports, and testify in court or before grand juries. The work is rigorous, physically demanding, and occasionally dangerous. ATF agents travel a great deal, and must be prepared for reassignment to different locations at any time. Some appointments may be overseas. Special agents start off at grade scale (GS) 5 and can be promoted up to GS-13. The ATF also hires investigators who perform investigations of alleged violations and various professional and technical workers such as attorneys, forensic scientists, and intelligence research specialists.

Border Patrol Agent

Border patrol agents work for U.S. Customs and Border Protection, the largest law enforcement agency within the Department of Homeland Security. Border patrol agents work to prevent people—undocumented immigrants, human traffickers, or terrorists—from entering the United States illegally. Agents spend much of their time on line watch, secretly watching land borders to see if anyone tries to cross them. They investigate cases by collecting leads and following up on them, flying over borders in aircraft, using electronic sensor television systems, and inspecting physical tracks left on the ground. Agents regularly visit farms and ranches, perform traffic stops, and patrol city streets to look for illegal immigrants. Border patrol agents must speak Spanish; if you do not already know the language, you will have to learn it at the border patrol academy.

Drug Enforcement Administration (DEA) Special Agent

Agents of the U.S. Drug Enforcement Administration work to fight the illegal production and sale of controlled substances, mainly illegal drugs. Agents try to stop drug trafficking by identifying the gangs that produce, import, and distribute them. Their tasks include carrying out surveillance of suspected drug traffickers, infiltrating drug distribution networks, and arresting those caught in criminal activities. The DEA requires its agents to relocate as necessary—signing a mobility agreement is a condition of employment. Extended temporary duty assignments away from home are common. Hours can be long and irregular, including many holidays, and the work can be quite dangerous. In addition to special agents, the DEA employs diversion investigators, intelligence research specialists, fingerprint specialists, and other employees.

Deputy United States Marshal

The U.S. Marshal Services enforce laws on behalf of the federal court system. The top officer in a federal district is called a U.S. Marshal; ordinary officers within the agency are called Deputy U.S. Marshals. Deputy U.S. Marshals protect federal courthouses and officers, transport prisoners, and seek fugitives from justice. They investigate crimes, conduct surveillance, arrest suspects when they find them, guard government officials, and seize assets held by criminals. Marshals catch gang members, people who have sexually assaulted children, counterfeiters, gun dealers, and many other types of criminals. New marshals start out at the GS-5 or GS-7 pay grade, and if successful will be gradually promoted up to the GS-12 level.

Federal Bureau of Investigation (FBI) Agent/ Special Agent

FBI special agents work to enforce federal laws and maintain national security. FBI agents conduct investigations of various different matters—terrorism, organized crime, cyber crime, counterintelligence, drug trafficking, air piracy, kidnapping, and many others. Agents meet with sources to gather information, search buildings for evidence of crimes, arrest criminal suspects, testify in federal court, and write up reports of their activities. New agents enter one of five career paths—intelligence, counterintelligence, counterterrorism, criminal, and cyber—and are sent to one of the FBI's 56 field offices. They generally spend three years in that first post and then move to another position. Agents can receive additional training throughout their careers and can often move up to managerial and executive positions. New special agents begin as GS-10 employees; the most experienced agents hold positions in grades GS-14, GS-15, and the FBI senior executive service.

Federal Air Marshal

Federal air marshals work for the Transportation Security Administration (TSA). They work to prevent attacks on U.S. air carriers, airports, and passengers. Air marshals spend their days walking through airports and riding airplanes. They must blend in with passengers, wearing ordinary clothes and acting like typical passengers, while spotting likely terrorists and planning ways of disabling them quickly. Air marshals must have good handgun proficiency. They are trained to recognize criminal behavior and to stop criminal acts within the tight confines of an aircraft. Air marshals are distributed among various law enforcement and homeland security organizations.

Immigration and Customs (ICE) Special Agent

U.S. Immigration and Customs Enforcement is the largest investigative agency in the Department of Homeland Security. It employs over 19,000 employees. Special agents, also called criminal investigators, conduct criminal and civil investigations into national security threats, commercial and financial fraud, drug trafficking, human trafficking, illegal arms deals, and other national-level problems.

U.S. Secret Service Agent

The Secret Service is best known for its work protecting the president of the United States, but it actually does much more. Many Secret Service agents spend their time investigating cases of financial fraud. The agency was originally founded to stop counterfeiting. Today's agents have expanded their skill set to include investigations of bank fraud, credit card fraud, and computer fraud. If you work for the Secret Service, you may spend much of your time interviewing the victims of financial fraud and researching networks of financial criminals. Of course Secret Service agents also investigate threats against the president and vice president, guard the White House and other federal buildings, patrol the streets of Washington, D.C., in marked vehicles, and other related tasks. A Secret Service special agent usually spends six to eight years in a field office, then three to five years on a protective detail. After that, he or she may move back to Washington, D.C., or move to another field office. Many

On the Cutting Edge

Wildlife Forensics

Do you like wild animals? You might consider the new field of wildlife forensics. Wildlife forensic scientists specialize in crimes done to (and sometimes by) wild animals. Various state, national, and international laws prohibit the hunting, capture, and sale of specific wild animals, but poaching is still a big and profitable business. People throughout the world like to buy wild animals (or parts of them) for pets, trophies and decorations, or as medicines. Wildlife forensic scientists are crucial to the international effort to stop the destruction of endangered species and the traffic in wild animal parts. If you go into this field you will have the opportunity to examine all types of evidence in warehouses and stores, such as purses made from reptile skins, meat from sea turtles, fur coats made from endangered mammals, ivory products from elephant tusks, jewelry made from rare shells, and medicines made from rhinoceros horns. You may even analyze hunters' clothing for blood.

agents spend part of their careers overseas. If you aim for a job in the Secret Service, you should have a college degree and several years law enforcement experience to begin with. As with all federal agencies, competition for jobs is stiff.

U.S. Secret Service Uniformed Officer

The Secret Service employs over 1,300 uniformed officers to take care of security at the White House, the residence of the vice president, the Department of the Treasury, and foreign diplomatic missions in Washington, D.C. Uniformed division officers patrol the city in cars, on foot, on motorcycles or bicycles, or man fixed security posts. The uniformed division includes the countersniper support unit, the canine explosives detection unit, the emergency response team, and a magnetometer support unit that uses metal detectors to inspect people entering secure areas.

Law Enforcement Positions in the Private Sector

While not affiliated with government agencies, these positions in the private sector offer opportunities to serve and protect the citizenry.

Security Guard

A security guard is employed by a company or business to protect people or property. Security guards are not sworn law enforcement officers, but they can sometimes perform law enforcement duties when ordered to do so by police, sheriffs' deputies, or other sworn officers. Security guards are often employed by private companies that specialize in providing security. They watch premises and do what they can to prevent crimes from occurring. Security companies usually train their employees in the use of weapons and restraints such as handcuffs.

University Public Safety Officer

Many colleges and universities have public safety departments devoted to preserving order on campus. Public safety officers handle campus parking and traffic issues, respond to complaints of crimes, shut down loud parties, provide crowd control during large sporting events, and take care of any other aspects of keeping students, faculty, and staff safe. Public safety officers are often sworn police officers who have all the training and authority of city police. Public safety organizations may work jointly with local police and sheriffs' offices to solve campus crimes.

Law Enforcement Positions with Post-Crime Investigations

When people think of law enforcement positions, they often neglect to consider those which contribute to post-crime investigations. While many of these jobs are performed in offices or laboratories, they are as essential in helping solve crimes as those performed in squad cars or on the street.

Artist/Sculptor

Did you think that law enforcement has no room for artists? Think again! If you can sculpt or draw, you might be able to get a law enforcement job that uses your skills. Crime victims can often describe their attackers in some detail. Police artists learn how to use those descriptions to create drawings based on those descriptions. Skilled artists with good descriptions can often render images that look quite similar to the actual individuals in question. Sculptors can use their skills in a slightly more ghoulish way. Sometimes law enforcement officials find bodies that have been dead for so long that they have decomposed to skeletons, and are very difficult to identify. Forensic sculptors can take a bare skull and reconstruct it by adding clay muscles and skin to create a plausible reconstruction of what the person might have looked like in real life. This can be very helpful for identifying remains.

Coroner/Medical Examiner

A coroner or medical examiner is an official who is in charge of examining the circumstances surrounding deaths and determining whether or not they are the result of criminal activity. This is usually a county-level office. Coroners are usually elected to their position and they do not necessarily need any medical qualifications. (Yes, this means that some coroners have no training or experience in medical examination. This is one reason many jurisdictions now appoint medical examiners.) Medical examiners are often appointed instead of elected and are required to be physicians with some training in forensic science. Coroners and medical examiners often function like detectives, asking questions about the circumstances of a death and examining the body for clues. They may be able to issue subpoenas to summon witnesses to testify. Depending on the state, coroners can write death certificates, issue search warrants, serve process, carry firearms, and handle other law enforcement duties.

Crime Analyst

Crime analysts collect data from police reports and other sources and use it to spot statistical patterns and create crime maps. This data is useful for predicting where crimes are likely to occur in the future. Crime analysts often focus on serial crimes, such as strings of thefts, rapes, or murders that seem to be connected with one another. Analysts often try to create profiles of likely suspects and come up with a description of the criminal's methods in order to identify likely suspects. A crime analyst can be either a civilian or a sworn law enforcement officer. Most crime analysts have bachelor's degrees and a good knowledge of computers, especially geographical information systems (GIS) software, and of statistical methods. If you like to work with numbers and computers, this could be an excellent field for you.

Criminalist

Criminalists identify and analyze physical evidence, such as blood, semen, DNA, hair, gasoline, footprints, and any other physical objects that can be left at a crime scene. As a criminalist, you may collect evidence yourself or analyze evidence brought from a scene by a detective or police officer. You may then process the evidence to separate out substances that are irrelevant to the case, such as separating animal hairs from human ones. A criminalist may compare a fired bullet with several guns to see which one was used to fire it, or check to see of a tiny slip of plastic came from a particular vehicle. The most important part of a criminalist's job is interpreting his or her results and producing a report that explains them clearly. Many criminalists begin their careers as bench scientists in laboratories, and gradually work their way up to directorial positions. Experienced criminalists may supplement their income by teaching at colleges. Criminalists can take a test to become certified by the American Board of Criminalistics.

Digital and Multimedia Specialist

Law enforcement is becoming increasingly high-tech. If you are an expert in digital photography, network analysis, or multimedia sciences, you will be able to find work in the field. Digital specialists take digital photographs of suspects, victims, autopsies, and crime scenes, produce computer images of crime scenes, create suspect composites, examine digital files and devices to see if they have been altered, examine audio and video recordings for accuracy, work with digital voice recognition software, examine computer files to see if information has been stolen or corrupted, and many other tasks that use computers and digital devices. Most people who work in this field have at least a bachelor's degree in computer science, information technology, or a related field. Some colleges and universities offer programs in digital forensics, computer forensics, and similar areas. Most large law enforcement agencies employ digital and multimedia professionals as computer-related crime investigators, speech scientists, image enhancement specialists, or general computer specialists.

Document Examiner

Document examiners examine documents and the materials and equipment that go into making documents. When an examiner looks at a document, he or she tries to determine who wrote it, whether or not it has been altered, whether anything has been added or erased, which pen or printer produced the writing, whether the signature is valid, what sort of paper was used, and similar questions. Document examiners consider letters, checks, wills and other legal documents, and any other example of text that could affect a criminal case. They use chemical and physical analysis to identify inks, toners, pencil marks, erasure residues, correction fluids, and papers. To get into this field, you will need a bachelor's degree, preferably in some scientific field. Most people begin their careers in an apprenticeship program in an area known as questioned documents under the direct supervision of an expert. An expert in this area would be a member of the questioned document section of the American Academy of Forensic Sciences. Documents experts work in most large law enforcement organizations; some also work in the private sector.

Forensic Dentist

If your career aspirations include both dentistry and law enforcement, you may not have to choose between them. You can go into forensic dentistry and have the best of both worlds! Forensic dentistry, or odontology, is the science of identifying people by their teeth or bite marks. Every person's bite pattern is unique, and most people today have dental x-rays on record. This makes it possible to identify human remains based solely on jaws and teeth, which are frequently the best-preserved parts of a skeleton. Forensic dentists also analyze bite marks on victims of violent crimes such as rape or assault, using the unique patterns to identify perpetrators. Most forensic dentists begin their careers as ordinary dentists and get specialized training in forensic dentistry. They will typically work with a more experienced forensic dentist until they learn the intricacies of the field. Forensic dentists often work as contractors or in formal appointments to coroners, medical examiners, military branches, and state and local government agencies. The American Society of Forensic Odontology (http://www.asfo.org) is a good source of information about getting into this field.

Forensic Scientist

A forensic scientist is a scientist who investigates crimes and legal issues. Forensic scientists come in many varieties: doctors, dentists, anthropologists, chemists, computer programmers, pharmacists, and many others. Their workplaces vary greatly depending on what they do. Some forensic scientists work in laboratories and have regular hours on weekdays. Others work out in the field, investigating crime scenes or the locations of accidents. They may be employed by police or sheriffs' departments, hospitals, toxicology laboratories, medical examiners' offices, or work as independent consultants. Some teach in colleges and universities. Forensic science is a great field for people who are extremely curious and love to solve puzzles.

Physical Anthropologist

What does a police department do when it finds a dead body in the woods? It calls a forensic anthropologist, of course. Physical anthropologists specialize in examining human remains, often in cases where those remains are so decomposed or damaged that no untrained individual could hope to identify them. Anthropologists study human skeletal anatomy to determine age, sex, health, age, and many other characteristics. They are skilled at determining how a person has died and how long he or she has been dead. Police departments and government agencies employ anthropologists to identify murder victims as well as people who die in fires, crashes, and other violent accidents that can leave bodies mutilated. Forensic anthropologists work as special agents for police departments and government agencies, for the armed forces, for state and local medical examiners' offices, and at universities and research institutions. If you want to go into this field, you will need to study biology, physical anthropology, and human anatomy, probably to a high level; many forensic anthropologists working in law enforcement hold Ph.Ds. The American Board of Forensic Anthropology (ABFA) certifies forensic anthropologists (http://www.theabfa.org).

Polygraph Examiner

A polygraph is a device used to determine whether or not a person is lying by collecting and assessing data about a person's physiological responses to questioning. Polygraph testing relies on the fact that most people exhibit signs of stress when they attempt to lie about something; they may sweat more than usual, their hearts may beat faster, and their blood pressure may increase. A polygraph machine consists of two metal plates that are attached to the subject's fingers to record sweat gland activity, and a blood pressure cuff that records the person's cardiovascular activity. A polygraph examiner hooks up a subject to the machine and then asks him a number of questions. Usually the examiner will begin by telling the person about the test and asking innocuous questions to establish baseline values. Questioning then proceeds to the details of the crime in question, while the machine records the subject's physiological activities. Afterward the examiner analyzes the data and comes up with an assessment of how truthful the person has been. Polygraphs are no magic bullet. Not every state admits the results of polygraphs as evidence in court, and many experts believe that polygraphs are not an effective means of reaching the truth. It is known that the validity of the results of a test depends very much on the examiner's skill and the care with which he or she prepares the examinee and analyzes the data.

Psychiatrist/Psychologist/Behavioral Scientist

There is tremendous need for psychological and behavioral services within law enforcement. Correctional institutions employ specialists in psychology or psychiatry to work with inmates and help them overcome the various mental ailments common in that setting. Forensic psychiatrists and psychologists work with lawyers and judges to determine the mental state of participants in criminal cases. Sometimes law enforcement officers themselves need psychological counseling or psychiatric treatment. If you go into any type of psychology, psychiatry, or behavioral science, you should find job opportunities within the law enforcement field, in hospitals, governments, or prisons. In order to enter any of these fields you will need at least a master's degree; psychiatrists, who can prescribe drugs to patients, are medical doctors.

Toxicologist

Are you good at chemistry? Do you find chemistry fascinating? Then you might enjoy working as a toxicologist. Toxicologists study the harmful effects of drugs and chemicals. Forensic toxicologists apply this field to legal questions, asking whether drugs, alcohol, or other chemicals might have contributed to deaths and accidents. Toxicologists usually work in laboratories, performing chemical analyses of body fluids and tissue samples and interpreting the findings. This analysis is often a crucial part of the investigation of crimes. Because samples are often very small, law enforcement toxicologists must be very skilled at their work. If you want to enter this field, you will need a bachelor's degree with a solid background in chemistry and preferably pharmacology. Some toxicologists have advanced degrees. Many people get into this area after working as pharmacists or laboratory chemists. Toxicologists work in police departments, law enforcement laboratories, medical examiner laboratories, hospitals, and universities.

Law Enforcement Positions with Courts and Corrections

Unlike a traditional beat cop, who is responsible for finding perpetrators and making arrests, those in these positions must be comfortable working with inmates over longer periods of time. In addition to traditional police skills, many of these positions require an ability to foster personal relationships with inmates and help provide the means for rehabilitation.

Bail Bondsman

Bail bondsmen make a living by posting bail for people accused of crimes in return for a percentage of the bail, often 10 percent of the total amount. The bondsman assumes the risk that the accused will jump bail and agrees to forfeit the entire amount if the accused does not appear at trial. If you go into this field, you will need a sizable chunk of capital and a high tolerance for risk. You will also have to be very careful about choosing your clients because some are more dangerous or untrustworthy than others. Bail bondsmen typically set up offices near courthouses or jails, where their customers can find them easily. Most states require bail bondsmen to hold licenses.

On the Cutting Edge

Licensing for Bail Bonding and Bounty Hunting

Licensing is a fairly new development in bounty hunting. A bounty hunting license gives an individual the right to hunt fugitives on behalf of a bail bondsman. Prior to the year 2000, anyone could re-arrest a defendant in most states; typically they had to register with a bail bondsman first, but otherwise there were no licensing or training requirements. Now many states have enacted laws requiring bounty hunters to receive training and register with the state, though not all states require bounty hunters to be licensed. These laws are constantly changing, so would-be bounty hunters must keep up-to-date with them. If you want to get into this field, check your state's requirements. In states that do require licenses, people who engage in bounty hunting without a license can be charged with a felony. Licensing laws also sometimes regulate the practice of bounty hunters who cross state lines in pursuit of fugitives.

Bounty Hunter

A bounty hunter is a person who uses the power of citizen's arrest to apprehend those who have been accused of a crime and who have skipped out on their bail and failed to turn up for their court dates. A bounty hunter is not a law enforcement agent and is not allowed to arrest anyone other than a bail jumper assigned to him or her by a bail bondsman, but bounty hunters do play an important role in law enforcement. Most states and bounty hunters have stopped using the term "bounty hunter," preferring more innocuous terms such as "bail enforcement agent," "fugitive recovery agent," or "bail runner." In recent years many states have begun licensing bounty hunters. Requirements vary from state to state. If you want to go into this field, you will need good investigative skills in order to locate your suspects and plenty of patience.

Correctional Officer/Detention Officer

Correctional officers work in jails and prisons, overseeing the people who have been arrested and are awaiting trial or who have been convicted of crimes and are serving sentences. Correctional officers maintain order by watching inmates and making sure they follow the rules. They may have to search inmates and their cells for contraband such as drugs or weapons, inspect locks and bars for signs that someone has tried to break them, and break up fights when they occur. Correctional officers keep daily logs of their activities, including descriptions of any disturbances that have occurred. Most correctional officers do not carry weapons but they do carry radios so that they can call for help if necessary. Correctional work is stressful and fairly dangerous; according to the Bureau of Labor Statistics, correctional officers have one of the highest rates of on-the-job injuries of all U.S. occupations. There are, however, many jobs available because jails and prisons must be staffed 24 hours a day, seven days a week.

Judge

A judge is an official who runs a court of law. Judges preside over trials, listening to testimony from both sides of a case and running the proceedings. In a bench trial, the judge or judges decide the outcome of the case. In a jury trial, the judge runs the proceedings but the jury decides the outcome. When they are not sitting in court, judges review pleadings and briefs that argue the different sides of lawsuits, meet with attorneys to set schedules, and write opinions explaining their reasoning in cases. The opinions of judges become part of the body of common law and serve as guidelines for attorneys and judges in future cases. There are many levels of judges, from magistrate judges who preside over small courts (often found in strip malls) to the justices of the state and federal supreme courts. Every state has its own conventions for selecting judges; some judges are appointed, while others are elected. Many judges spend part of their career as trial lawyers before moving to the bench.

Probation/Parole Officer

Parole officers supervise people who have served prison sentences and been released but who are still on parole. Probation officers supervise people who have been convicted of crimes and have been sentenced to probation instead of prison. In both cases, the job involves keeping track of convicts and helping them stay out of trouble. Officers meet with their charges regularly, get to know their families, help them find jobs or training, visit them at home or at work, and arrange for substance abuse treatment if necessary. Officers also work for the courts, investigating the backgrounds of their charges and recommending sentences. This work involves close contact with people who have committed crimes and their friends and families. Officers must be prepared to handle angry and even violent people, and must be good at dealing with stress.

Prosecutors and District Attorneys

Prosecutors are attorneys who prosecute people who are accused of crimes. They meet regularly with law enforcement officers and judges to decide how to handle the accused. They gather evidence, argue cases in court, enter into plea bargains, and propose sentences. Most counties have their own prosecutors. Different states call their prosecutors by different names. Many states call them district attorneys, or DAs. Others call them prosecutors. In South Carolina, county solicitors are in charge of prosecuting alleged criminals. Some states have a district attorney who oversees criminal prosecutions throughout the state. Depending on the state, head prosecutors or district attorneys may be elected or appointed by an elected

executive, such as a governor. These attorneys then staff their officers by hiring lower-level attorneys, paralegals, and other staff.

Public Defender

Public defenders are attorneys who defend people accused of crimes.
Many accused individuals are too poor to hire attorneys themselves.
Because every American citizen is guaranteed a defense attorney if
accused of a crime, states, counties, and cities have created various
ways of providing public defenders. Some states have public defenders' offices and pay attorneys to work full time defending poor
defendants. In some cases, public defenders and prosecutors receive
about the same salary, which is almost always less than the attorneys working there could receive in the private sector. Attorneys in
the Federal Public Defender's Office are paid fairly well. Some states
do not employ public defenders and instead assign indigent defense
cases to the attorneys who belong to the state bar on a pro-bono
basis.

Warden

A warden or superintendent is the chief officer in charge of a correctional institution. If you work for several years as a correctional officer, gain experience in corrections, and have good leadership ability,
you might aim for a job as a prison warden. A warden handles all the
administration of a prison. This includes hiring and firing correctional officers, setting budgets, determining what correctional policies the prison will use, setting rules and regulations, and handling
serious disciplinary matters. The job can be challenging because
inmates can be difficult to handle and funding for prisons is often
less than needed. Most wardens have at least some college, and
many have advanced degrees. The position of warden often comes
with free housing (important if the prison is far away from cities and
towns) and the use of a vehicle, which makes it a fairly desirable last
job in a law enforcement career.

Chapter 4

Tips for Success

If you work in law enforcement and public safety, your first priority will be making sure that you and your colleagues get home in one piece every day. This job can be dangerous; never let a quest for advancement get in the way of keeping yourself alive.

That being said, much of succeeding in law enforcement is a matter of common sense. Follow the rules, come to work on time, be polite to everyone, and offer to help as much as possible. If you do those things, you can have a successful career. Moving up will require more of you—specialized training, a college degree, passing tests, or years of experience—but those too should be accessible to anyone with some wherewithal and common sense.

Succeeding in Law Enforcement and Public Safety

If you want to succeed and move up through the ranks in law enforcement, you will have to find a way to stand out. Most officers will gradually take on more responsibility as they gain experience and new officers arrive, but if you want promotions to the higher ranks you will have to do more than just the minimum required of you. The first thing you can do to enhance your chances of moving up is to do a good job with your work and stay out of trouble. The following tips may seem obvious, but they bear repeating:

➡ Come to work on time. If you are late, you will at best inconvenience your co-workers and at worst put co-workers or citizens in danger.

➡ Be polite. Be polite to co-workers so they will be willing to help you with daily work and recommend you for promotions. Be polite to lay people so that they will think well of the police.

➡ Follow the rules and try to stay out of trouble. Officers who violate procedures can get entire departments into hot water. When superiors look for candidates for promotion, they tend to overlook troublemakers.

➡ Offer to help. Go above and beyond the strict call of duty. Volunteer for overtime or extra duty.

➡ Learn all you can. If your department offers training, take it. Superiors look for officers who are willing to enhance their skills when handing out promotions.

➡ Make connections. Promotions often happen internally. One of the best ways to land plum assignments is to have superiors or co-workers go to bat for you.

➡ Try to like what you do. People who enjoy their work tend to be successful at it; people who hate their jobs have a much harder time succeeding. If you decide you really hate law enforcement, try to change something. Maybe you need another assignment. Maybe you need to leave law enforcement entirely. It is not for everyone.

Promotion is the result of experience, seniority, on-the-job performance, and written test scores. It also comes from other people's opinion of you. If your superiors and co-workers see that you do a good job with your work and that they can rely on you, they will help you get good assignments. Law enforcement depends on good teamwork; be a good team player!

Getting Into Law Enforcement

The good news is that law enforcement and public safety agencies are hiring. Demand for officers at all levels is high, and will continue to be high as the population increases. What do recruiters look for? They want to find recruits who look likely to succeed as police officers. They want people who are responsible, friendly, well-spoken, decisive, and hard-working. Most jurisdictions require recruits to pass a written test and get through a training program, which takes care of the academic and physical side of things, but recruiters really want to find people who will be where they are supposed to be at the right time. Law enforcement officers rely on their colleagues for backup, and the public relies on them for much of its protection. When talking to a recruiter, you want to come across as someone who would be reliable in a tight spot or a dangerous situation.

Prepare a résumé that showcases your accomplishments. Make the most of what you have done. You may think you have not done much with your life so far, but you have almost certainly done something that will impress a recruiter. Even if you are coming straight out of school and have never held an impressive job, highlight your accomplishments. Were you president of the drama club or secretary of your fraternity? Have you spent hours volunteering in a local soup kitchen? Make yourself look energetic and organized.

Life experience is extremely valuable to law enforcement officers, and may be even more important than education. Most recruiters love to see candidates who have done something besides live in their parents' homes and work part time jobs. Law enforcement officers must be able to make quick decisions that may be matters of life and death or put large sums of money on the line. Recruiters want officers who are mature. Even moving into your own apartment while you go to college can help make a case that you are grown-up enough to handle law enforcement decisions, but concrete work and volunteer experiences are probably better. Summer or part-time jobs that involve responsibility for people or property, such as working as a camp counselor, can prepare you for work in law enforcement. Even better is a history of work in paying, challenging jobs, especially the military.

Networking is one of the most important things you can do to get a job and to move up through the ranks. Networking is often the best way to find jobs, since jobs are never advertised at all but are the result of referrals. While it is true that many law enforcement jobs are advertised, networking can definitely help you in this field, and it is easier than it sounds. Anyone you know can be part of your network of contacts. Good friends, casual acquaintances, old teachers, employers, and distant relatives can all be part of your network, and you never know when one of them might help you land a job. Online forums and social networks can help, but do not neglect the real world for the Internet! Law enforcement is a job that requires its officers to get out in public and interact with real people.

City, County, and State: Getting In and Moving Up

Follow these precepts to begin your journey towards a state or local law enforcement career.

Police Officer Selection Test

Most police jurisdictions require applicants to pass a test before admitting them to police academy. These tests vary from state to state, but generally they are designed to ensure that candidates can read, write, calculate, and think well enough to function as law enforcement officers. The National Police Officer Selection Test (POST) is one of the most common. It tests applicants on arithmetic, reading comprehension, grammar, and report writing. The questions on the test are related to police tasks. Standard and Associates, the company that produces the test, claims that high scores on the POST correlate with good performance in police training, which is why jurisdictions use this test or other similar ones to pre-screen applicants.

Do not be alarmed at the prospect of taking a written test. The POST is a difficult test, but it is possible to improve your chances of getting a good score by studying. If it has been years since you took math, practice working some problems. Go over vocabulary words likely to be on the test. As a police officer you will need to be able to communicate effectively with a wide variety of people, so a good vocabulary is essential. You will need to read at a 10th through 12th grade level; if this is a problem, you may be able to take a remedial class or work with a tutor to get up to speed. The POST also tests map reading, another skill essential to working as a law enforcement officer.

The best preparation you can do is working problems from actual POST tests. Some jurisdictions supply applicants with study materials. Get a practice test and work through it. Time yourself. When you take the actual test, you will only have 15 or 20 minutes per section, so get used to those time limits before you sit down with the real thing. If you do not understand a question or a section, get someone to help you.

The night before the test, try to get a good night's sleep and avoid alcohol. Get to the test center early so that you will have time to get settled and visit the restroom before the test begins. The test administrator will explain how the test works; if you do not understand something, ask questions *before* the test begins. Once you start working on the test, try not to get distracted. Focus on the test. If you get nervous, take deep breaths and try to relax. Remember, lots of people get terrified by tests, so if this happens to you, you are not alone. Regardless of how you feel, answer every question. There is no penalty for guessing, and a guess has a better chance of being correct than no answer at all.

Police Academy Requirements

Most law enforcement officers go through some sort of training such as a police academy before joining the force. This applies to both city police and county sheriffs' deputies. Every state has its own requirements for entering training and being hired by a police force. To get the best information, check with your state or city's police departments to see what one must do to become a law enforcement officer.

Everyone
Knows

Vital Technology

Law enforcement agencies need officers who understand technology. Experts in computers and other high-tech devices are highly desired by police and sheriffs' departments and other law enforcement agencies. If you are going to college before starting a job in law enforcement, consider taking some computer classes, either as a major or just as electives. If you are already an officer or civilian employee of a law enforcement agency, you can take night classes and become the expert your department needs. Technology is a great area to volunteer services and expertise; departments often do not realize that they are lagging behind the times and administrators simply do not have the time to worry about upgrading computers. If you offer to do regular upgrades and troubleshooting and keep the office equipment running smoothly, your superiors will quickly decide that you are indispensable.

INTERVIEW

Your Mission Is To Go Home After Every Shift

Beth Lavin
Deputy, King County Sheriff's Office, Seattle, Washington

How long have you worked in law enforcement?
Nineteen years.

What jobs have you held?
Property crimes detective, master police officer, field training officer, school resource officer, member of active shooter team.

How did you get into law enforcement?
I remember as a little girl that I always wanted to be a police officer. I remember telling my grandparents when they asked what I wanted to do that I wanted to be a "poweece officer." Helping people, always interacting with people was who I was. I was a protector as well with my sister and mom, so it felt natural to become a police officer. I first went into the U.S. Army when I was 17. I wanted to get life experience and get the discipline I needed. The military was a stepping stone for me to get into law enforcement.

What tips would you have for a person just starting out in a career in law enforcement?
To keep an open mind, be a sponge. You're going to get a whole lot of

In general, states set physical and educational requirements that would-be officers must meet before being hired by a police department or being allowed to enroll in a police training program. Qualifications may include a background check to see if you have any history of criminal arrests; taking an examination such as the Federal Civil Service Examination or a test of literacy and receiving a passing grade; and passing a physical examination that assesses physical conditioning through running, push-ups, and sit-ups. Most states require applicants to be over a minimum age, such as 21, and under a maximum, such as 45. Large police departments in big cities sometimes hire high school graduates in their teens as trainees or cadets. These young people do clerical work and attend police information and training during the start of your career. Try not to get down on yourself. If you make a mistake, learn from it and move on. Your mission and goal is to go home after every shift.

What are the most important qualities a person needs to succeed in a law enforcement career?
Be able to adapt to anything that comes your way. Communication is key to being successful. A lot of this job is common sense. You also need honesty, integrity, and compassion.

What does a person need to do to advance in law enforcement? Is a college degree important? What about other specialized training?
To advance, I would say, go to training classes or conferences that would enhance your career. It's so important to invest in your career, even if you have to pay for the training yourself. I would rather have someone that has a ton of life experiences and street experience than promote someone just with a college degree. Specialized training is key as well—being a field training officer, [you] get involved with community policing. It really depends on what you're looking at in the law enforcement field. For instance, if you want to get into K9, then volunteer to do quarries (as training targets for police dogs, quarries wear bite suits to protect them and pretend to be criminals so that the dogs can practice taking them down) and go on ride-alongs with the K9 unit. Being a team player is also key to getting ahead in your career.

academy or criminal justice classes until they are old enough to become uniformed officers.

Many states and cities run police academies that train all new local officers. States often have multiple police academies, some of them operated through community colleges and others run by law enforcement agencies. Some police academies are residential, and trainees are required to live on campus during their training periods. In several jurisdictions, you must be hired by a police department before you can attend the academy. In that situation, the training is typically free of charge and the trainees are paid full salaries during training. In other cases, trainees must find their own jobs after finishing their training. In a number of states, certification as a law enforcement officer is contingent on a graduate's finding a job within a certain time period, such as one year; if an individual does not find employment within that time, he or she may have to undergo a refresher course to be re-certified.

Police academies train new officers in all the skills they will need on the job. Students spend a good deal of time in the classroom. They study the law surrounding law enforcement, including types of crimes, federal and state laws governing crimes, evidence, laws of arrest, and search and seizure. They also learn how to arrest and book suspects, how to conduct investigations and write reports, traffic investigation and enforcement, and radio and communications equipment. Most academies include some training on human relations, including cultural sensitivity, stress management, media relations, sexual harassment, domestic violence, and similar topics. Many academies include language training, especially Spanish. Outside of the classroom, students practice all the basic skills they will need on the job. They learn advanced driving skills, including defensive driving, pursuit, and safe vehicle handling. They study tactics, including vehicle stops, building searches, patrol techniques, shooting policies, and how to handle crimes in progress. Firearms training covers weapon safety, gun care, marksmanship, use of side-arms, shotguns, and weapons such as Tasers, and the handling of chemical agents. Trainees also work to get themselves into good physical shape and practice physical arrest techniques. Academies may offer advanced training in other topics, such as mobile field force tactics, bomb squad, community policing, and air support operations.

Application Requirements and Training

Each state police agency has its own process for choosing and training new recruits. Check with your state to see what it requires. The California Highway Patrol (CHP), for example, requires applicants to be between 20 and 35 years of age on the day they take their written test. Candidates must have 20/20 vision either with or without correction, normal color vision, and good physical and mental health. All applicants must hold either a high school diploma or GED or pass the California High School Proficiency Examination. An associate's degree or higher is very desirable. The force particularly wants its officers to be proficient in math, English reading and composition, and computer use. Foreign language skill is especially useful.

Highway patrol officers can have no prior felony convictions and must possess a valid drivers' license with a relatively clean traffic history. All officers must be U.S. citizens. Permanent resident immigrants who have applied for citizenship are welcome to apply, but they cannot become officers until they have become citizens.

The California Highway Patrol trains its officers in the CHP cadet academy. Cadets spend six months at this live-in facility, which can house 480 students. There they dress in uniforms and work, eat, and room with their future colleagues. They are given time off on Wednesday evenings and weekends, assuming they pass their tests satisfactorily. The training is paramilitary: Cadets practice military-style drills so that they can participate in ceremonies and function efficiently in tactical formations for quelling riots. Cadets study a number of academic subjects, including agency policies and procedures, criminal law, and accident investigation. All cadets undergo military-style physical training and practice enforcement tactics such as proper use of force, patrol techniques, and vehicle pullovers, weapons training, emergency vehicle operations training, pursuit and defensive driving, and training in CHP customs and courtesies. Once a cadet enters the academy, he or she receives monthly pay and medical benefits.

Criminal Justice Programs Enhance Career Options

Many people earn degrees in criminal justice as a way of entering law enforcement or enhancing their prospects for promotion. Some law enforcement agencies want their applicants to hold at least an associate's degree in criminal justice or a related field. Others allow people to apply with just a high school degree or GED, but some college will definitely help your chances of getting a job.

Criminal justice programs are quite common at technical colleges, community colleges, and universities, so you will probably be able to find a program near you. You can earn all levels of degrees, including two-year associate's degrees (A.A. or A.S.), four-year bachelor's degrees (B.A. or B.S.) and master's degrees that take a year or two of study beyond a bachelor's degree.

Pay and career options are strongly correlated with level of degree; people who hold the most advanced degrees can make the highest salaries. Of course there is a tradeoff in time and money. If you want to get started in your career quickly, then earning the degree that

Professional
Ethics

Handling Discrimination

Imagine you are a police lieutenant. One of your female patrol officers comes to you and reports that one of her male co-workers is bothering her. She says he asked her out a few weeks ago and she said no. Since then he has made a number of comments about her body, brushes up against her when they pass in the hall, and once left a condom sitting on her car seat. This all started after he asked her out and she refused him. Now she says she is frightened of him and does not believe she is safe working with him on patrol. Do you a) call in the male officer and discipline him, knowing that you risk alienating a valuable officer? Or b) move the female officer to a desk job on a different shift and in a different office, which would get her out of the male officer's path?

If you guessed B, you might have just opened up your department for a lawsuit. Moving the female officer could be considered retaliation for bringing a complaint of sexual harassment. If an employee complains of any sort of discriminatory treatment, it is his or her supervisor's duty to investigate it and stop it in a way that does not harm the victim. If you advance into the supervisory ranks, you will almost certainly encounter cases of sexual harassment and racial discrimination, which still occur despite laws against them and sensitivity training. Take all complaints seriously; discrimination destroys morale and can result in legal liability for the department.

costs the smallest amount of money and takes the shortest time is your best bet. Remember, you can always go back to school as your career progresses. Associate's degree credits often transfer to bachelor's programs, so classes you have already taken may count for your next degree.

A number of colleges offer online degrees in criminal justice. This is a good option for people who do not have the time to attend classes in person and who are good at working independently. Keep in mind that you will need lots of self-discipline if you go this route.

The study of criminal justice encompasses several fields, including criminology (the study of criminals and crimes), law, the court system, psychology, sociology, forensic science, and correctional theory. Studying criminal justice is a good way to learn the theoretical basis for much of law enforcement, as well as the practical side of the profession. You will also study English composition, college math, and probably some science such as biology or chemistry, which is useful for gathering evidence.

College can be expensive. If you already have a job with a law enforcement agency, it may pay for your courses and then pay you a higher salary after your degree is complete. Otherwise, there are various ways to handle the cost of college. Some people work while taking classes in order to pay their tuition. Some borrow the money from the college or a family member. Many states offer tuition assistance and scholarships to qualified students; visit the college financial aid office to find out if you are eligible.

The Military Route

Many law enforcement officers entered the field after spending time in the U.S. military. Police and sheriffs' departments like veterans because they already have many of the skills officers need —discipline, firearms skills, and experience in working under pressure. If you are a veteran, you might go ahead and apply for law enforcement positions without a criminal justice degree or other college degree. The military can also provide you with money for college.

Internships Open Doors

One of the best ways to get into law enforcement is to get an internship with a police department or other agency. The Federal Bureau of Investigation; the Bureau of Alcohol, Tobacco, and Firearms; and the Drug Enforcement Agency all run internship programs for high school and college students and introductory programs for recent college graduates. Many city police departments also have college internship programs. Some college criminal justice programs can arrange internships with local law enforcement agencies. There is a wide range of programs available for students, some of them paid and some not.

Law enforcement agencies go out of their way to make sure interns stay safe. As an intern, you will probably find yourself watching more than doing, though good programs will ensure that interns can do some real work. Internships are a great way to see what it is really like to work in an area. They are also a terrific way to make connections with potential employers; if you do a good job as an intern and impress your superiors, they will be more likely to hire you for a permanent position.

Advice for Novice Officers

During your first months as a police officer or even while you are in training at the academy, your best ally may be your field training officer, or FTO. Police and sheriffs' departments throughout the United States use FTOs to ease new recruits into the reality of police work. FTOs spend much of their time guiding new officers, making sure they stay alive and keeping them out of trouble.

Many new officers fall prey to certain pitfalls. They have completed the police academy and are full of their new knowledge, and want to make sure everyone else realizes how much they know. This is not good. To maximize your chances of pleasing your superiors (which, after all, is your key to advancement), you should keep certain things in mind:

➡ The officers who run the police academy are real police officers and have experience working out on the streets. The fact that they are teaching in the academy does not make them less than "real" cops.

➡ Your FTO knows what he or she is doing and is worthy of respect. You may be younger and more plugged in, but your FTO knows more about police work than you do.

➡ Do not become "badge heavy," or so impressed with the fact that you are a police officer that you get arrogant about it. A law enforcement officer will do much better by respecting people in the community than by showing lots of attitude.

➡ Respect your supervisors and behave yourself at work. Superior officers generally do not appreciate cocky attitudes and sarcasm from rookies. Follow the chain of command.

➡ Follow departmental procedures. They exist for a reason. If there are rules about memorizing general orders, studying local maps, cleaning your firearms, and writing reports, learn them and follow them.

➡ Remember that law enforcement is a dangerous business. You study survival skills and officer safety at the police academy because law enforcement officers, no matter how safe their beats, are *always* at some risk. Take safety seriously.

Problem Solving

Shoot or Don't Shoot?

Imagine that you and your partner are gang enforcement officers with the Los Angeles Police Department. You are on patrol around midnight when you see a man in his 20s approaching your patrol car. You notice that he is looking around in what could be a suspicious manner, and he is fumbling with his waistband. You cannot see him too clearly because it is dark. You yell at the man to stop so that you can see what he is up to. Instead of stopping, he walks toward you quickly and appears to pull something from his waistband. Do you shoot or not?

Law enforcement officers face this situation daily. If the suspect is pulling a gun, you need to stop him before he shoots you. But what if you shoot him and it turns out that he was not only unarmed but autistic, and you and your partner killed him with your well-aimed simultaneous shots at his head? That is a disaster. Expect your department's internal affairs division to conduct a thorough investigation, in which you will have to explain everything that went through your head that night, especially your legitimate and imminent fear for your life. You may be taken off patrol and given desk duty while the investigation proceeds. If the department finds that you engaged in misconduct, you may receive a reprimand or a suspension. Expect to receive protests from concerned citizens and groups such as the American Civil Liberties Union, who may publish articles complaining about police brutality and abuse of power and publicly criticizing you by name. You may have some sleepless nights; it is never pleasant to discover that you have killed an innocent person. Finally, you need to accept that you will make mistakes, and that the nature of your work means that you may occasionally hurt people or even kill them.

Paying Your Dues

No one moves up in law enforcement without paying their dues. You may think you are too talented to waste much time with police academy and patrol duties and want to go straight to detective work or the SWAT team. You may think you could be a great law enforcement officer but only want to work daytime hours during the week, no nights. You may think it would be great if you could be the youngest police chief your department ever has; you are so smart, surely everyone will agree that you should be promoted as quickly as possible.

Law enforcement does not work that way. It is a hierarchical profession and promotions depend very much on putting in the right amount of time at each level. You will never advance without putting in lots of time and hard work. Almost all officers start out on uniformed patrol, and many of them put in years there. This is the case in nearly every law enforcement organization, from federal agencies to small-town city police. Patrol is where you learn the basic skills of law enforcement work: how to deal with co-workers and the public, how the department works, how to write reports, and how to keep the public safe without endangering yourself or your fellow officers.

You actually do not want to move up too quickly. It takes a long time to gain enough experience to handle supervision. Remember, a supervisor must keep his or her underlings safe. The skills you learn in patrol apply to every level of police work, and more experience on patrol will only enhance those skills. Experience also plays a role in departmental rankings for promotion. No department will recommend that you be promoted to sergeant with only a few months patrol experience; you simply would not be ready for the work.

Spend your early days learning how your particular department works. Ask veterans how they moved up. Learn about other career paths, such as moving from police work to federal law enforcement. And concentrate on doing a good job with your day-to-day work. Your early days on patrol are part of your education as an officer, and will provide you with the opportunities you will inevitably encounter in the years to come.

Many law enforcement officers aspire to become detectives. This can be a slow process. Law enforcement agencies generally promote detectives from the ranks of patrol officers, and require these officers to have a certain amount of experience before applying. If you want to become a detective, the best thing to do is to spend time with the detectives already on the force. Learn what they do and try to imitate it in your own work. Get to know your superior officers and try to impress them with your performance.

Departments rank their officers on a promotion list. Sometimes promotions are tied to specialized training. If you are interested in specializing in a certain area such as vice, narcotics, SWAT, or juvenile affairs, be sure to tell your superiors so that they can help you when positions open up. Many higher ranks require officers to hold bachelor's or master's degrees. If you aspire to the better-paid positions with more responsibility, you will need at least a four-year degree. Language skills are very useful to police officers in certain areas. For example, Spanish has become an extremely common language in Florida, California, and other parts of the United States, so law enforcement agencies especially want to hire officers who can speak Spanish.

Promotional Tests

Law enforcement departments often require officers to pass tests in order to move up to detective, sergeant, or other higher ranks. Officers may need to make a minimum score to qualify for promotion. They may be ranked for promotion according to the scores they achieve. Without a good score on the test, you can kiss your chances for promotion goodbye.

Law enforcement exams include written and oral portions. The written questions test your knowledge of law enforcement principles and your ability to answer multiple-choice questions under pressure. Oral questions can be even more stressful, because they require you to think on your feet in front of a panel of examiners.

Tests also include practical exercises, such as an in-basket exam. An in-basket exam consists of numerous documents introducing you to a hypothetical law enforcement case such as one that might face a police lieutenant or captain. You first study the background information, work scenarios, organizational charts, schedules, and other documents that might apply to a real-life case. You are then presented with a hypothetical case in the form of several documents in an "in-basket." You have a short amount of time (such as 90 minutes) to analyze the situation, write up a report, and answer questions about how to handle the case. The test evaluators are looking for your comprehension of the situation, your ability to communicate effectively in writing, your ability to plan and assess risks, your decisiveness and delegating ability, and your initiative.

Any time you find yourself facing a test, find out what is on it and study for it! Few people can pass tests without at least some idea of what to expect. There are many commercial test prep books and online training programs available, and these can be quite helpful if you put in some practice time with them. Ask your colleagues which ones they recommend for your department.

Financial Survival

Law enforcement officers make decent salaries, but you should not enter law enforcement expecting to get rich. Most veteran officers augment their paychecks by working lots of overtime or by holding jobs on the side; it is not unusual for officers to double their take-home pay with extra work. Overtime pay is governed by either a federal law called the Fair Labor Standards Act or by a union contract. A typical overtime rate is 1.5 times the worker's hourly rate for hours worked beyond 40 in one week. To get overtime, you can work extra shifts; provide security at parades, fairs, football games, or other events that need law enforcement; or go to court to provide security or serve as an expert witness. Some officers find part time work as security guards for apartment complexes or companies.

Not every employee is eligible for overtime. The Fair Labor Standards Act divides employees into exempt and non-exempt workers, as in "exempt from overtime pay." Generally employees who are considered management and administration are exempt, which means they are not eligible for overtime. In law enforcement, lieutenants and captains may be considered exempt. It is possible for a lieutenant, who has a higher salary than a sergeant, to make less money than that sergeant because the sergeant is eligible for overtime pay and the lieutenant is not. Consider that when you apply for promotion!

Remember to look at the whole picture when considering your financial situation. Many departments pay recruits going through the police academy, though many do not. Some buy uniforms for their officers. You may get benefits such as health insurance, college tuition reimbursement, flexible spending accounts, pay incentives for specialty training, and other perks. Most importantly, do not live beyond your means. The temptation of easy credit is an easy way to get into debt. Overtime work is not guaranteed; many officers have grown to depend on overtime pay only to fall into financial ruin when it dried up.

Best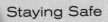
Practice

Staying Safe

There is no getting around the fact that law enforcement and public safety are dangerous jobs. So how do veterans stay safe? They follow certain rules, and are always thinking of a backup plan. Consider the following standard practices:

- Make sure your weapon will work for you. Does your gun work? Is it loaded, and do you have enough ammunition? Most importantly, keep up your skills at a consistently high level. Go to the shooting range regularly to practice loading and shooting and do malfunction drills. Know which weapon you want for a given situation; rifles and shotguns are usually better choices than handguns.

- Carry a backup weapon and extra magazines and ammunition.

- Wear body armor on patrol. It will not help you if you do not wear it.

- Expect to be attacked. You never know when a call for help will turn out to be an ambush. Coming to the scene of a robbery or assault can be risky, and domestic violence calls are known to be dangerous to officers. (Some couples stop fighting each other and attack the officer.) Be ready to move quickly and aggressively.

- Stay in shape. You may need all your physical strength and agility to handle rough situations.

- Cultivate alliances with your colleagues. Discuss possible scenarios and possible responses to them. Learn what sort of weapons and other gear they favor.

- If you get shot and you are not dead yet, do not give up! Keep on fighting. Your partners should be there to help you.

- Wear your seatbelt. Car crashes are a more common risk than gunfights. (Of the 109 officers killed in the line of duty in 2008, nearly two-thirds of them died in vehicular accidents.)

Landing a Federal Law Enforcement Position

Federal law enforcement positions are among the hardest to land. The FBI, the ATF, the U.S. Marshals, and the DEA all have very strict admission requirements and typically hire fewer than 5 percent of qualified applicants. Those hired tend to have four-year college degrees and at least four years of police or military experience. They are also physically fit, have clean criminal records, and no history of drug use.

U.S. Marshals Service

To become a U.S. Marshal, you must be a U.S. citizen between 21 and 36 years of age (you must be appointed before your 37th birthday), have a bachelor's degree or three years of qualifying experience, have a valid drivers' license and a good driving record, pass a background investigation and structured interview, and be healthy and physically fit. If you pass those requirements, you must attend the U.S. Marshals Service Basic Training Academy at the Federal Law Enforcement Training Center in Glynco, Georgia. New deputies spend 17 and a half weeks studying legal and courtroom procedures, evidence, defensive tactics, firearms, first aid, driving, officer survival, search and seizure, prisoner search and restraint, computer use, building entry and search, surveillance, and other topics. New officers are hired as Police Series GL-082 Deputy U.S. Marshals. Note that GL-082 refers to the career track that U.S. Marshals follow, based on the federal law enforcement officer series of pay grades and perhaps switching to the general schedule after a few years. Most USMS officers spend a year as GL-5, a year as GL-7, three years at GS-9, and are then promoted to GS-11 or GS-12.

Before you can attend the U.S. Marshals training academy, you will have to pass a physical fitness test. This is intended to ensure that you will be physically capable of handling the intense physical demands presented by training and by law enforcement work, including daily runs of up to 10 miles. So get in shape before you show up!

The U.S. Marshals schedules regular information sessions for would-be deputy marshals; check the agency's Web site to see the schedule of information sessions. Local recruiting officers can also provide information. The hiring process can take 10 months or longer. The agency sends its deputies wherever it needs them, and all candidates must sign a mobility agreement promising to go where they are sent, though the USMS does try to place applicants within the region in which they apply.

You may be able to enter the U.S. Marshals through the Federal Career Intern Program (FCIP), which is designed to attract exceptional individuals to careers in federal agencies. If you join the U.S. Marshals through this program, you will spend two years working in a trial period, but work as a Deputy U.S. Marshal the whole time—not as a student intern as the program's name might suggest. This program can also serve as a fast track into criminal investigator status (GS-11), which would make you eligible for LEAP pay.

Federal Bureau of Investigation (FBI)

To enter the FBI, you will need to be accepted into the FBI Academy. New trainees spend 21 weeks at the academy in Quantico, Virginia. There they undergo training in firearms, defensive tactics and the practical application of investigative techniques. They spend many hours in class studying federal law, terrorism and counterterrorism, criminal investigation, national security, and related topics. After successful completion of the course, graduates are sworn in as FBI Special Agents.

Physical fitness is extremely important for FBI Special Agents, and trainees are required to pass a physical fitness test before leaving the academy. The test is given in the first week of the course. Trainees who fail are put in a remedial program for extra training and are not allowed to leave the academy overnight until they take the test again in the seventh week. Those who fail the physical fitness test at this point are dismissed from the academy.

Drug Enforcement Agency (DEA)

The Drug Enforcement Agency wants applicants to be between 21 and 36 years of age. In addition, an applicant must have a valid driver's license, a good credit history, a favorable work history, and no prior felony convictions. New agents must successfully complete a 19-week basic agent training program at the DEA Training Center in Quantico, Virginia. New agents must satisfactorily complete a one or two-year trial period before being formally appointed to the DEA.

The DEA, not surprisingly, is particularly adamant that its employees be drug-free. Before the DEA will even consider an applicant, he or she must pass a drug test, complete a questionnaire that shows complete compliance with DEA drug policies, and pass a background investigation. For some positions, employees will need a top-secret security clearance.

Bureau of Alcohol, Tobacco, and Firearms (ATF)

Like agents for other federal agencies, ATF agents must hold a driver's license, comply with the ATF drug policy, and be physically fit. The ATF actually specifies that an agent's weight "must be in proportion to height." ATF applicants must pass a drug test, a polygraph test, and a background investigation for a top-secret security clearance. ATF applicants must also pass the Treasury Enforcement Agent (TEA) examination and the ATF special agent applicant assessment test. The ATF has very strict requirements for eyesight and hearing, at least for its field agents. Special agents must have uncorrected vision of at least 20/100 in each eye, and corrected vision of at least 20/20 in one eye and 20/30 in the other. They must have good depth perception, peripheral vision, and color vision. Hearing loss must be minimal. All applicants must undergo a medical examination to make sure that their senses measure up.

The ATF's training program for special agents is one of the longest of the federal agencies. New agents spend 27 weeks at the Federal Law Enforcement Training Center in Glynco, Georgia. They study marksmanship, explosives, arson techniques, organized crime and terrorist practices, methods of stopping smuggling, and other specialized criminal investigation techniques that apply to alcohol, tobacco, and firearm violations.

Fast Facts

Selective Service

Have you registered with the Selective Service? If you are male and want a job in federal law enforcement, you had better make sure you have. In order to be eligible for federal employment, all males born after December 31, 1959, must prove that they have registered with the Selective Service System or be exempt from having to register for some reason. There are very few exemptions for men. Men who were born as women and underwent sex changes are exempt, as are foreigners temporarily in the United States, such as students. Men currently on active duty in the U.S. military are also exempt, as are students at the military service academies. Women are not required to register.

U.S. Immigration and Customs Enforcement (ICE)

To enter the ICE as a Special Agent, you will either need a four-year college degree or at least three years of law enforcement experience with evidence of increasing responsibility during that time. ICE Special Agents are paid according to the GL pay scale, the federal pay scale for certain law enforcement officers. The higher your grade number, the higher the pay you will receive. To enter at the GL-5 level, you would need to have experience gathering data, analyzing problems, planning and organizing work, and communicating well in speech and writing. If you have more experience or higher degrees, you may be able to enter at the GL-7 or GL-9 level. Superior academic achievement in the form of a high GPA or class rank is an advantage.

ICE employees must be U.S. citizens who have either lived in the United States for three out of the past five years or worked for or been a dependent of the U.S. government or military. People who have been convicted of particular crimes are not eligible for employment with the ICE. All applicants must undergo a structured oral interview and a writing test. As with most federal positions, you must be physically fit, under the age of 37, willing to move, and able to carry a firearm. All ICE Special Agents must complete a 22-week paid training program at the Law Enforcement Training Center in Glynco, Georgia.

Secret Service

Secret Service agents spent 11 weeks at the Federal Law Enforcement Training Center in Glynco, Georgia, followed by an additional 16 weeks of training in Washington, D.C. In Georgia they study firearms use, defensive tactics, federal and state law, and report writing. The specialized training in Washington, D.C., includes advanced driving techniques, how to spot counterfeit money and credit card fraud, and physical protection. Officers who join the countersniper team that is positioned on the roof of the White House undergo more specialized training in long-distance shooting and long-range threat detection.

The application process for the Secret Service is very competitive. You will enhance your chances if you have several years of law enforcement experience with an emphasis on criminal investigation or a four-year college degree with excellent grades. The Secret

Service is especially interested in recruiting special agents who speak foreign languages fluently. If you can pass a test of general professional proficiency in a language, you will be eligible for a one-time recruitment bonus equivalent to 25 percent of basic annual pay.

Forensics and Polygraph Work

To become a forensic scientist, you will need at least a bachelor's degree, preferably in a scientific discipline such as chemistry, biology, mathematics, physical anthropology, or forensic science. You will want to get very good at taking notes, possibly in the field. You should also take a number of classes in English composition or some other subject that will give you plenty of experience in writing papers. Good public speaking skills are very valuable.

The most important qualities a forensic scientist can have are precision, attention to detail, objectivity, and the ability to communicate clearly in written reports and in spoken testimony. If you work in a laboratory, you will need to keep your equipment meticulously clean and in good working order. You will need to keep specimens very carefully organized and identified; many cases have fallen apart because the evidence was not stored or labeled properly. Simple ingenuity is crucial for succeeding in this field; physical evidence sometimes comes in miniscule quantities and can be very difficult to analyze, and interpreting results to reconstruct a crime is difficult. It is very important that the forensic scientist not jump to conclusions without basing them on solid evidence. After all, a person's life may hang in the balance.

Most forensic scientists have bachelor's degrees, and many of them have master's or professional degrees as well. Many of them take continuing education courses throughout their careers. Polygraph examiners learn their art in one of about 20 polygraph academies and institutes located throughout the United States. Reputable schools are certified by the American Polygraph Association. Many states have organizations of certified polygraph examiners and only accept as members people who have adequate training. Joining the American Polygraph Association is a good idea and may be essential if you want to work in this field. The organization is a useful source of training, job leads, and connections.

Chapter 5

Talk Like a Pro

The world of law enforcement uses a variety of distinct terms. Often these have special or very specific meanings. When is a "bench" more than a bench? What is the difference between burglary and theft? From old English to Latin terms and phrases, the sweep of legal vernacular gathers many far-flung concepts. Whichever part of the law enforcement field may interest you, it is important to master its specific jargon. Knowing a bit about the terms used by colleagues in other specialties is always a good idea. See the glossary below for a cross-section of what professionals in the industry need to know.

accuse To charge someone with a crime; to institute legal proceedings against a suspected criminal.

accused Someone charged with a crime.

active shooter An armed person who is in the act of using deadly force, such as shooting a gun; usually an active shooter has already attacked a victim and has access to more victims; a sniper.

adjudicate To judge; to formally issue a final judgment in a court proceeding.

administrative agency A governmental organization that implements a particular piece of legislation, such as workers compensation or tax law.

admissible Acceptable; valid; able to be admitted. Admissible evidence is evidence that is proper to admit at trial because it is relevant to the matter at hand.

adversary proceeding   A hearing or trial with opposing parties, one seeking relief from the other, and that ends with one party receiving a favorable outcome at the expense of the other.

advocacy   Pleading or arguing for a cause. Trial advocacy is arguing for a cause in court as part of a trial.

affidavit   A written declaration of fact(s) made under oath and signed by the author.

affirm   To confirm; state as fact; ratify; to declare that a previous judgment is correct. "Affirmation" is the act of confirming that something is true; affirmation can be used as a substitute for an oath in the case of religious or ethical objections to swearing.

affirmative action   Deliberate and positive efforts to help victims of discrimination by remedying effects of past discrimination and preventing future discrimination.

affirmative defense   In pleading, a response to a complaint that constitutes a defense and justification for defendant's actions instead of attacking the truth of plaintiff's allegations; affirmative defenses include self-defense and insanity.

aforesaid   Said earlier; previously mentioned.

aforethought   Premeditated; planned in advance.

aggravate   To make worse.

aid and abet   To knowingly help someone to commit a crime.

alias   A fake or alternate identity. Also used to indicate the use of a false name, e.g. "Samuel Clemens, alias Mark Twain."

alibi   A defense in which the defendant claims to have been someplace other than the scene of a crime when the crime was committed and produces evidence to prove it, thus proving that it was physically impossible for him or her to have committed the crime in question.

allege   To claim; to assert; to state in a pleading what one intends to prove at trial. An "allegation" is the act of stating that a person has committed a particular act or that a particular event has occurred.

amend   To fix; to improve; to modify or revise a document.

amicus curiae   Latin for "friend of the court;" someone who is not a party to a lawsuit but who has a strong interest in the subject matter of a case and petitions the court for permission to file a brief providing information on the matter to aid the court in rendering its decision.

amnesty   An official pardon granted by a government to a group of people forgiving them for past crimes, usually political crimes such as treason or draft evasion.

appeal   To request a higher court to review a case that has been decided by a lower court and render a new decision, either a reversal or a new trial.

appeals court   A court that can hear appeals; also called a court of appeals or an appellate court.

appear   To come into court as a party to a lawsuit and submit to the court's jurisdiction appearance.

appellant   One who files an appeal.

appellate   Having to do with appeals.

appellate court   A court that reviews decisions made by lower courts and does not hear new cases.

appellee   The party against whom an appeal is filed; the party who prevailed at trial in the lower court.

arraign   In criminal law, to bring a defendant into court, charge him or her with an offense, and allow him or her to plead.

arraignment   The first step in the criminal process, in which a defendant is called into court, charged with a crime, informed of his or her rights, and allowed to plead guilty or not guilty.

arrest   To use legal authority to deprive someone of liberty; to stop someone suspected of a crime and take him or her into custody.

arrest record   The official record of times a person has been arrested.

arson   The crime of intentionally and maliciously setting property on fire.

assault   To attack physically; to threaten or attempt to cause injury to someone else. When contact occurs, the offense is often called assault and battery.

award   To grant something; money or other object given as a grant or compensation; also the decision rendered by a non-judicial decider such as an arbitrator.

bad check   A check written on an account with insufficient funds to pay it or on a closed account.

bad faith   Deceit; intent to defraud; dishonesty in dealing with someone.

bail   Money or other security given temporarily to the court to allow a prisoner to be released before trial and to ensure that he or she will return for trial; if the prisoner does not return for trial, he or she forfeits the bail; to furnish money or property to get someone released from prison on bail.

bail bond   A contract between a prisoner, the state, and a third party known as a bail bondsman, in which the bail bondsman agrees to furnish bail for the prisoner in return for a fee and takes the risk that the prisoner will not return for trial.

bailiff   (1) A court officer who keeps order and looks after jurors and prisoners. (2) An agent or steward who is responsible for property or goods.

bailiwick   A bailiff's jurisdiction.

bankruptcy   A process in which a court declares a person or business insolvent and orders the debtor's assets to be sold to pay off creditors, at which point the debtor is discharged from any further obligation and may begin anew. Chapter 7 bankruptcy is a proceeding that liquidates property, pays off debts, and leaves the debtor discharged. Chapter 11 bankruptcy is a business reorganization, in which a court supervises an insolvent business while it continues to operate and comes up with a plan for reorganization.

bench   (1) A court; the seat a judge occupies in a courtroom; the office of judge. (2) The collective body of judges.

bench warrant   An order issued by a court for the arrest of a person, often used to make that person appear in court.

beyond a reasonable doubt   Criminal case terminology which indicates that a case is proven by evidence that a reasonable person would be entirely convinced and morally certain proves the guilt of a defendant.

breaking and entering   Forcibly opening a building and then entering it; two elements of the crime of burglary.

breathalyzer   A device used to check the level of alcohol in a person's breath; breathalyzer test results are admissible as evidence.

brief   (1) A written document presented to the court and to opposing counsel by a lawyer describing the facts of a case, questions of law, and legal arguments in support of his or her client's position. (2) A summary or abstract of a case. Can also be used as a verb meaning (1) to write a summary of a case, or (2) to inform someone of the details of something.

burglary   Breaking into and entering a building with intent to commit a crime (usually theft) once inside. Traditionally, the breaking and entering had to occur at night. Today this requirement varies from state to state.

capital offense   An offense for which execution is a possible punishment; also called a capital crime.

capital punishment   The death penalty; punishment by death.

carnal knowledge   Sexual intercourse.

case   (1) A legal action or lawsuit to be decided in a court or law or equity. (2) The legal arguments and evidence used by one side of a lawsuit to support its position.

cause of action   A set of facts that creates a valid legal claim that can be grounds for a lawsuit.

challenge   To object; to dispute the truth of a statement.

chamber   A hall or room in which a judicial or legislative body meets.

chambers   A judge's private office.

circumstantial evidence   Evidence drawn from inference or deduction; secondary evidence.

citation   A summons issued by a court ordering its recipient to appear in court at a specified date and time.

citizen   A legally recognized member of a nation or state, who owes allegiance to the government and in return receives the government's protection.

civil action   A lawsuit brought by a private citizen to protect a private or civil right or to seek a civil remedy; a non-criminal action.

civil court   A court handling civil actions, i.e., non-criminal matters.

civil liberties   Personal rights and immunities from government oppression established and guaranteed by the Constitution, including freedom of speech and freedom of association; natural liberties that cannot be limited by the government.

civil rights   The rights of all citizens to personal liberties, freedom, and equality; rights specifically granted through laws enacted by communities, as opposed to civil liberties, which are rights that the government is not allowed to restrict.

clerk   A court officer who keeps court records, files pleadings and motions, issues process, and enters judgment.

client   An individual or organization that employs a professional to provide that professional's services; someone who employs an attorney to represent him or her in court, to draft legal documents, to advise, or to provide other legal services.

closing argument   An attorney's final arguments to the judge and jury at the conclusion of his or her case, summing up the facts supporting the case and explaining why the opposing side's case is inadequate.

code   A systematic collection of laws, regulations, or rules. Examples of codes include the civil code, which is the collection of laws based on the French Napoleonic Code that governs

Professional
Ethics

The Necessity of Due Process

Say you catch a man in the act of murdering his girl-friend because she tried to break up with him. You get there too late and she dies, but at least you know the guy will go to jail. You and a whole bunch of other people watched him do it. Why even bother with a trial? Due process of law, that is why. Due process of law is the fair judicial treatment guaranteed to every U.S. citizen by the Constitution in the Fifth and Fourteenth Amendments, which promise that no citizen will be deprived of life, liberty, or property without the opportunity to first defend him or herself. This includes the right to a fair trial, to be present at one's trial, to be allowed to present testimony and to present evidence to counter the opposing side's case. So even if you think the case is clear-cut, the guy gets his day in court.

Louisiana jurisprudence, and penal codes, which are collections of laws dealing with criminal acts and punishments.

cold case A crime or incident that occurred long in the past, has not yet been solved, and is no longer the subject of active investigation.

common law A system of law based on judicial precedent and custom rather than statute and code; the system of jurisprudence used in England and most of the United States.

complaint In criminal law, a charge made before a magistrate that a particular person has committed an offense, in an effort to begin the process of prosecution.

conflict of interest An ethical dilemma in which a person is entrusted with two duties at odds with one another, and where attention to one duty will harm the other.

convict For a court to find someone guilty of a crime. Also used to refer to a person who has been found by a court to be guilty of a crime.

conviction The legal act of finding someone guilty of a crime; the end of the prosecution, including the judgment or sentence.

coroner A public official who investigates sudden, violent, and suspicious deaths.

correctional institution   A jail, reformatory, prison, or other institution where those convicted of crimes are sent.

correctional system   The government system of correctional institutions and parole systems.

corroborate   To confirm or verify; to agree with or support.

counterterrorism   Efforts made by a law enforcement agency or government to stop the acts of terrorists.

court   A tribunal in which a judge and/or jury hears and decides civil and/or criminal cases; the governmental entity that applies the state's laws to cases and controversies and administers justice. Also called a court of law.

creditor   A person or business to whom a debt is owed.

criminal   One who commits a crime; one who violates a criminal law. Also used as an adjective meaning related to a crime, expressing something done with malice or intent to injure.

criminal law   The branch of law that deals with the prosecution and punishment of criminals; the body of law that determines what constitutes a crime and what constitutes suitable punishment.

criminology   The academic study of crimes and criminals, including motivations and methods.

cross-examination   At trial or a deposition, the examination of a witness by the opposing party, regarding testimony already raised on direct examination and matters of witness credibility.

CSI   Crime scene investigation, especially investigation that uses forensic science to interpret evidence.

custody   (1) Responsibility or guardianship of a person or thing. (2) Imprisonment.

damages   Money awarded as compensation for injury or loss.

death penalty   Capital punishment; punishing someone for a serious crime such as murder by killing him or her.

debtor   (1) A person who owes a debt to someone else. (2) A person subject to bankruptcy proceedings. A judgment debtor is someone who is the subject of a judgment awarding a sum to a creditor.

decedent   Someone who has died.

decide   To come to a conclusion or resolution after deliberation and consideration; to determine something.

decision   A conclusion reached after considering facts and applicable law if necessary; a judicial determination or judgment.

decree The judicial decision of a court in equity made after hearing testimony and determining the rights of the parties, equivalent to a judgment by a court of law, though the term judgment may also be used in reference to courts of equity.

de facto Latin for "in fact," used to describe a situation that exists. The term is typically used to describe situations that exist without legal or official approval.

defendant The party against whom a lawsuit is brought: in civil cases, the party who responds to the complaint; in criminal cases, the person against whom charges are brought.

defense attorney An attorney who normally represents defendants in lawsuits.

de jure Latin meaning "by law, by right"; the condition of being in compliance with all applicable laws; legitimate and lawful.

deny In pleading, for the defendant to contradict the allegations made in the complaint, to state that the plaintiff's allegations are not in fact correct.

deport To send a foreign national from one country to another because he or she has committed a crime or is of illegal immigration status.

deposition A form of discovery before trial in which an attorney questions a witness under oath and a court reporter makes a transcript of the testimony, which can then be used as evidence at trial.

deputize To give a person the power to exercise the functions of a superior's office and to act on the superior's behalf, such as a county sheriff's granting power of law enforcement to a deputy.

deputy An agent; a substitute; someone empowered by a superior to exercise the functions of the superior's office and to act on the superior's behalf.

deputy sheriff An officer who has the authority to exercise the duties of the office of sheriff.

discrimination Unequal or unfair treatment of people based on categories such as sex, race, religion, or age, when by all rights they should be treated fairly.

dismiss (1) To allow to leave or send away. (2) To terminate someone's employment. (3) For a judge to refuse to consider a lawsuit further, thereby ending it before a trial is completed.

dismissal A judge's order that terminates a lawsuit or motion without considering the issues involved in the matter.

district attorney A public officer of a state or county whose duty is to prosecute those accused of crimes within the area; different states use different titles, including prosecuting attorney, county attorney, state's attorney, or solicitor.

district court   (1) A federal court that has jurisdiction over a particular region of a state and hears cases arising out of offenses against federal laws and cases involving litigants from different states. (2) In some states, an inferior court with general jurisdiction over minor matters.

docket   (1) A list on a court calendar of cases scheduled to be tried. (2) On appeal, a formal record summarizing the proceedings of a lower court.

double jeopardy   A second prosecution for an offense after the defendant has already been tried for it and acquitted; prohibited by the Fifth Amendment of the Constitution.

driving under the influence (DUI)   Operating a motor vehicle while under the influence of alcohol or drugs; also called driving while intoxicated (DWI) or drunk driving.

duress   Conduct intended to force someone to do something they do not want to do, such as threat of violence or coercion.

dwelling   A residence; a house, building, or any enclosed space or structure used as a home; a house and all buildings attached to it.

equal protection (of the laws)   The principal that every person is entitled to the same treatment under the law as other people in similar conditions.

equal protection clause   A clause in the Fourteenth Amendment to the Constitution that prohibits states from denying people within their jurisdictions equal protection of the laws.

Esq.   An abbreviation for "esquire," often used to identify individuals who are licensed to practice law by having been admitted into a state bar. The correct usage is as a suffix, such as "Jane Doe, Esq."

evidence   Anything used to prove the truth of an issue in court; includes testimony, documents, objects, and anything else that could persuade the jury.

fact finder   The person or group of people whose job is to determine the facts in a case; also called the trier of fact.

family court   A court with jurisdiction over matters related to families and children, including child abuse and neglect, support and custody, paternity, and juvenile delinquency.

federal courts   The courts of the United States, created by the Constitution or by an act of Congress and having jurisdiction created by statute, including federal district courts, federal courts of appeal, and the Supreme Court of the United States.

Federal Rules of Criminal Procedure Procedural rules created by the Supreme Court in 1945 that govern proceedings in criminal cases before U.S. district courts and sometimes before U.S. magistrates.

Federal Rules of Evidence Rules governing admission of evidence before U.S. district courts, U.S. magistrates, and bankruptcy court, and that have been used as a model for rules of evidence by many states.

felony A serious crime. Most felonies are defined by statute, and often include those that are punishable by death or by more than one year of imprisonment.

finding A court's or jury's conclusion about a matter of law or fact. A finding of fact is a court's or agency's determinations about the facts of a case after hearing testimony, examining evidence, and deliberating. A finding of law is a court's determination of how to apply law to the facts of a case.

forensic science The science of investigating crimes and crime scenes.

fraud Intentional misrepresentation of the truth done to cause someone else to rely on that misrepresentation and be deceived into surrendering a legal right or otherwise being injured.

gainful employment A job or occupation that earns money or generates profit; employment for pay that is suited to the abilities of the worker; also called gainful occupation.

gamble To bet; to play games of chance for money; a risky enterprise that could turn out either a profit or a loss.

gambling Betting; playing games of chance for money.

game Wild animals that can be hunted.

game laws Federal and state laws that regulate the hunting of animals for sport or food.

garnish To seize someone's money, property, or wages to settle a debt or claim.

good faith Sincerity, honesty, lack of deceit; a sincere intention to do what is promised.

graded offense A crime that has different degrees and penalties depending on level of guilt. For example, a murder can come in first, second, or third degree.

graft Corrupt practices used by public officials to unlawfully take public money; money obtained by corruption.

grand jury A group of people who are selected to investigate an alleged crime and indict suspected criminals.

green card A registration card that allows a permanent resident alien to live and work in the United States.

guardian A person who looks after the legal and financial affairs and/or takes care of someone who is unable to because of age or disability.

guilt The condition of having committed a crime or wrongful act.

guilty Having committed a crime; culpable; having been determined by a jury to have committed a specific crime.

guilty plea A voluntary admission of having committed a crime made to a court by a criminal defendant, punishable in the same was as a guilty verdict after trial.

gun control law A law regulating sale, possession, and use of guns and firearms.

habeas corpus Latin for "you have the body;" a writ that institutes a court proceeding to determine whether a criminal defendant has been lawfully imprisoned, or to test the constitutionality of a conviction; also used in cases of child custody and deportation.

hearing A legal proceeding, usually less formal than a trial, in which the parties to a case are given an opportunity to present evidence and testimony to a judge or other official who determines the facts and makes a decision based on the evidence presented.

hearsay A report made by a witness of something that another person said or communicated nonverbally, usually not admissible as evidence.

holding A court's ruling on an issue presented at trial; a legal principle produced by a court in deciding a case.

immunity Exemption or protection from something such as prosecution, duty, or penalty.

imposter Someone who pretends to be someone else with the intention of deceiving others, usually to gain some benefit.

impound To seize and take legal custody of something, such as a vehicle.

imprison To put in prison; to keep someone restricted to a place that essentially functions as a prison; to confine; to deprive of liberty.

incarcerate To put in jail or prison; to imprison.

incriminate To suggest or charge that someone is guilty of a crime.

incriminating evidence Evidence that helps establish the guilt of an accused person.

inebriate To make intoxicated or drunk.

infamous crime Historically, a crime that renders its perpetrator infamous; under the modern view, a crime punishable by death or imprisonment in a state penal institution for more than one year.

injunction A court order prohibiting someone from doing a specified act in order to prevent future injury.

inmate A person confined to a prison, a hospital, or other institution.

innocent Not guilty; in good faith; without intention of committing a wrong or knowledge that a wrong is being committed.

John or Jane Doe A generic name used to name a party to a lawsuit when that party prefers to remain anonymous, or to refer to an individual whose name is not known, such as a dead body without identification. Sometimes the surname "Roe" is used instead of "Doe," as in Roe v. Wade.

judgment (1) The ability to form opinions and make decisions. (2) The court's final decision in a trial; the amount of money awarded to the prevailing party by the court. A final judgment is a judgment that ends a legal controversy by conclusively stating whether or not the plaintiff is entitled to relief.

Fast Facts

K9 Units

Everyone knows that K9 units are units that use service dogs, or canines. K9s perform huge variety of tasks, and police forces around the world have found that different breeds have different skills. Many stereotypical "police dogs" are German shepherds, chosen for their strength and intelligence, which makes the ideal for protecting officers and bringing down criminals. Other breeds favored for this work are rottweilers, boxers, Doberman pinschers, and giant schnauzers. Bloodhounds, with their extremely sensitive noses, are the classic search and rescue dog. Cute little beagles also have keen noses; police use them to sniff out drugs and as cadaver dogs, to find dead bodies. Other sniffing specialists include basset hounds, cocker spaniels, English springer spaniels, and Labrador retrievers.

judicial   Related to the office of judge, judgments, the administration of justice, or courts; related to the interpretation and application of laws.

judicial authority   The power that comes as part of the office of judge; the power to hear cases and render decisions. Also called judicial power.

judicial branch   The branch of government consisting of courts and other entities that exist to interpret and enforce laws.

jurisdiction   (1) The power to make judicial decisions; a court's or judge's power to investigate the facts of a matter, apply law to them, and declare a judgment. (2) The territory in which a particular court can exercise its authority; the system of courts within a particular area.

juror   A member of a jury.

jury   A group of people selected and sworn to hear the evidence in a case and decide what the true facts are, usually composed of a cross section of the community.

jury trial   A trial that takes place before a jury, in which the jury hears the testimony and sees evidence and then renders a decision about the facts in accordance with the judge's instructions.

larceny   Taking the property of another person without the owner's consent and with the intention of making it the property of someone else.

lawsuit   An action at law or equity; a dispute brought before a court for determination.

lawyer   An attorney; a person who has studied law or who practices law.

mafia   a body of organized criminals who use extortion, threats, and violence to influence business or government. See organized crime.

mafioso   A member of the mafia.

magistrate   A public official with judicial, executive, or legislative power granted by the government, often functioning as a judge over minor matters or as a justice of the peace.

magistrate's court   A court over which a magistrate presides, handling small claims and minor matters.

malfeasance   Bad conduct; wrongdoing; a wrongful or unlawful act, particularly by a public official.

malice   Evil intention; an intention to do a wrongful act or commit a crime without any justification or excuse.

malice aforethought A state of mind in which a person deliberately plans to commit a crime before actually performing it, characterized by cruelty and a disregard for the consequences to human life and social duties.

malicious Intending to do harm; done out of ill will and without justification.

malum in se Latin for "bad in itself"; describes an act that is inherently wrong in itself without regard to what the law says.

malum prohibitum Latin for "bad because it is prohibited"; describes an act that is wrong because it is prohibited by law.

manslaughter the act of killing someone without premeditation, either accidentally or after provocation.

marshal a public officer who enforces laws; the head of a police or fire department; a sheriff.

martial law government by the military instead of civilians during times of war or extreme civil unrest.

material essential; important; relevant to establishing a cause of action or arriving at a judgment.

mens rea the mental state that occurs when committing a crime, such as the guilt, criminal intent, or knowledge that a crime is being committed; one of the four mental states in which a crime may be committed: intentionally, knowingly, recklessly, or negligently.

misconduct Improper behavior; neglect of duties; mismanagement.

miscreant A person who breaks a law or a rule; a person who behaves badly.

misdemeanor A minor crime, less serious than a felony and usually punished by less severe penalties.

misrepresent To make a false or inaccurate statement; to give the impression by words or behavior that a situation is different from what is in fact the case.

mistrial An invalid trial; a trial terminated before a judgment is reached due to circumstances such as a hung jury, lack of jurisdiction, or other fundamental problem.

mitigate To make something less severe or serious.

modus operandi Latin for "way of operating"; a way of doing things, especially used to refer to a criminal's habitual methods. Also called m.o.

moral turpitude Depravity, dishonesty, or vileness; conduct that grossly violates acceptable standards of morality and acceptable behavior.

motion   A formal application to the court asking for a rule or order in favor of the applicant, such as a grant of summary judgment, dismissal of a complaint, or a new trial.

motive   The reason for doing some act; the idea or circumstances that cause someone to do something.

municipal   Related to a city or town or its government, or other local government; occasionally used in reference to state or national government.

murder   The unlawful killing of a person by another person with malice aforethought. First-degree murder is an unlawful killing that is willful, deliberate, and premeditated. Second-degree murder is an unlawful killing without deliberation or premeditation but with malice aforethought. Serial murder is the murder by one killer of several victims over a period of time.

mutilate   To injure badly; to deprive someone of the use of a limb; to inflict serious, disfiguring damage on someone or something; to damage or alter a document so that it becomes imperfect.

narcotics   Drugs based on morphine or morphine-like substances that can relieve pain and cause general loss of feeling and interest in life. Regularly abused narcotics include heroin, morphine, codeine, and other painkillers.

negligence   Failure to use the proper care in doing something, or the amount of care that an ordinarily prudent person would use under the same circumstances.

notary public   A person with the authority to perform a limited range of legal functions such as administering oaths, witnessing signatures, drawing up contracts or deeds, or taking depositions.

oath   The act of swearing that something is true; a promise to tell the truth in court or perform some act, often sworn before a witness or invoking a supreme power. The expression "under oath" describes an act done after swearing an oath.

oath of allegiance   An oath binding its taker to some nation or leader.

oath of office   An oath sworn upon taking some office, promising to perform the office properly.

obscene   Morally offensive; against accepted standards of decency, especially in a sexual way; appealing to sexual interests and without serious political, literary, scientific, or artistic value.

obstruction of justice   Hindering the process of justice in court or of judicial acts, such as by influencing jurors or preventing an officer of the court from performing his or her duty.

occupant   A person who occupies a property; a person who possesses and uses property.

offend   To commit an illegal act; to break a rule.

offender   One who commits an illegal act.

offense   An illegal act; an act that violates criminal laws; a felony or misdemeanor.

officer   (1) A person who holds an office. (2) A member of the armed services with authority to command. (3) A member of the police force. (4) A person entrusted with the management of a corporation.

official   A person who holds an office; with the authority of a public body; done by an officer.

opening statement   A speech made by an attorney at the start of the trial describing the facts and issues and arguments that the attorney will make.

opinion   A statement written by a judge explaining his or her decision in a case.

organized crime   A systematic, large-scale crime organized and executed by professional criminals; often racketeering. The criminal organization known as the mafia engages in organized crime.

oyez   A word meaning "hear ye" that is cried by a bailiff to mark the beginning of a court session; pronounced "oh yes."

parole   The release of a convict from prison before the end of the sentence on the condition that the former prisoner follow certain rules and commit no more crimes.

parolee   A person released from prison on parole.

parole officer   An official who supervises parolees.

party   A person or entity involved in some transaction or matter; a person or entity on one side of a lawsuit or other dispute.

perjury   The crime of intentionally lying under oath during a judicial proceeding, such as at trial.

plea   In criminal law, a defendant's response to the charges brought against him or her.

plea bargain   An agreement made between a criminal defendant and the prosecutor in which the defendant agrees to plead guilty to a lesser offense in exchange for a lighter punishment after conviction.

plead   In criminal law, to answer charges brought by the prosecution.

pleading   A document containing a party's side of a lawsuit, such as a plaintiff's complaint or a defendant's answer, in which the party lists the facts that support his or her side of the case and presents them to the court at the beginning of a lawsuit.

precedent   A previously decided case that serves as a guide for deciding subsequent cases that have similar facts or legal questions.

prejudice   Bias; prejudgment not based on actual experience or evidence; injury to a party that results from preconceived notions about the facts.

prima facie   Latin for "first face" or "at first sight"; based on first impressions; the initial view of something, accepted as true until disproven.

prima facie case   An initial case; a case with sufficient proof to stand trial and withstand a motion to dismiss or for a directed verdict, and that will be accepted as true until the defendant proves otherwise.

prima facie evidence   Evidence sufficient to establish a claim or defense until rebutted by contrary evidence.

probation   A sentencing procedure where instead of imprisoning a person convicted of a crime, the court releases him or her to the supervision of a probation officer with the understanding that a violation of the terms of probation will result in a prison sentence.

proceeding   A lawsuit or legal action; a step or event that is part of a lawsuit; a hearing, inquest, investigation, or other action that takes place before a judicial officer.

proof   The use of evidence or argument to establish a fact; evidence offered at trial to show the truth of some proposition.

pro se   Latin "for oneself;" appearing on one's own behalf; describes a person who represents himself or herself in a lawsuit.

prosecute   (1) To begin legal proceedings against someone, especially by the state against an accused criminal. (2) To continue to carry out some action intending to complete it.

prosecution   The act of prosecuting; the party prosecuting a case.

prosecutor   An attorney who prosecutes criminal cases on behalf of the state.

public defender   An attorney employed by the government to represent criminal defendants who cannot afford to pay for a lawyer.

racketeering   Engaging in a conspiracy to commit business fraud, extortion, or coercion; using threats to extort money, goods, or services from business owners.

ransom   A sum of money or other valuable item demanded for the release of a prisoner, especially a kidnapped person.

rape   The crime of having sexual intercourse with someone without his or her consent and against his or her will; also called sexual assault.

rebut   To respond to an argument or claim with contrary arguments and evidence; to refute.

rebuttal   The opportunity given to a defending party to respond to and refute the arguments presented by the party presenting a case in chief, or to the party who initiates closing argument after the other party has responded to that argument; an oral argument responding to and refuting an initial case.

recess   A break in a court or legislative session in which official proceedings are suspended for a short time.

recidivist   A repeat offender; a person who habitually and regularly commits crimes.

record   An official written report about some event or transaction; written documents, audio and video tapes, and other documentary information.

rehabilitate   To restore a person or business to a normal level of health, freedom, reputation, dignity, finances, or other capacity; to help a criminal improve his or her situation so as to abandon crime in the future.

remand   (1) For an appellate court to send a case back to a lower court for reconsideration. (2) To place someone in custody, such as a defendant while a trial is adjourned.

reprieve   The temporary postponement of a criminal sentence.

sanction   (1) Official approval of some action. (2) A penalty or threatened penalty for disobeying a law or rule; penalties taken by one nation against another, such as trade restrictions, intended to force it to comply with some standard.

search   To look for something; to explore hidden places in a person's house, vehicle, or other place in a quest for evidence of a crime.

search and seizure   A search in which the officers conducting a search take evidence of a crime if they find it.

search warrant   A written order issued by a judge or judicial official in the state's name, authorizing a sheriff or other officer

Best
Practice

The Miranda Rule

If you catch a criminal in the act of committing a violent crime—say, you catch him murdering his girlfriend by stabbing her with a butcher knife—and you cuff him, throw him in the squad car, and drive him to the station, will he be sure to go to jail? You know the answer to this one: He will not go if you forget to read him his rights. A procedure called the Miranda warning is a rule requiring that before a person is interrogated about a crime, he or she must be informed of legal protections against self-incrimination and the right to counsel. The Miranda rule has been federal law since the 1966 case *Miranda v. Arizona*, in which a man confessed to a crime during a rough interrogation. The Supreme Court ruled that interrogating the man without informing him of his right not to testify against himself violated the Fifth Amendment's protection against self-incrimination. Evidence obtained from questioning done without first reading the Miranda warning is inadmissible in court. Though the rule exists to protect all citizens from abusive arrests by the government, having a case fall apart because of a technicality can be a bitter pill to swallow. The states and federal government have since refined the Miranda requirements, and at this point officers in some states are allowed to require suspects to identify themselves during police stops without having to be read their rights.

of the law to search a particular place for evidence of a crime and to seize it if found.

seize   To take someone's property by force; for a police officer authorized by a search warrant to take the real (i.e., land or buildings) or personal (i.e., movable objects such as money, jewelry, or vehicles) property of someone who has broken the law or who has been ordered to forfeit that property by the court; to take a person into physical custody.

self-defense   The act of defending oneself against threatened injury; the right to protect oneself or one's family from immediately threatened harm, which can serve as a defense in a criminal or tort action arising out of injuries caused by an act of self-defense.

self-incrimination The act of testifying against oneself or implicating oneself in a crime, which the Fifth Amendment forbids the government to require of anyone.

sentence The punishment given by the court to a criminal defendant who has been found guilty of a crime.

separation of powers The division of the U.S. government and many state governments into three branches—executive, legislative, and judicial—each of which wields a particular set of powers unique to it and not shared by the other branches, and which the other branches are not permitted to use.

sequester (1) To isolate; to separate or segregate; to hide away; to isolate a jury during a trial. (2) To seize property pending the outcome of litigation or to hold until a debt is paid; to impose spending restrictions on a government; to declare someone bankrupt. Also called sequestrate.

serve To deliver a legal document such as a summons in an official capacity.

service The act of working for someone; the work that is performed by someone.

service of process The formal delivery to a defendant of the complaint, summons, or other legal document that notifies him or her that a lawsuit has been brought.

settle (1) For the parties to a lawsuit to resolve their dispute on their own before a court reaches a final judgment on the matter after trial, thereby allowing the trial to be cancelled and the lawsuit terminated. (2) To dispose of finally, such as after death; to give property to someone.

sex crime A crime involving sex, either with a sexual motive or involving a sexual act such as rape, sexual assault, or indecent exposure.

sex offender A person who has been convicted of a sex crime.

sexual abuse Illegal sexual contact between a minor and an adult.

sexual assault Forcible sexual contact inflicted on an unwilling victim.

sheriff An officer elected by a county to keep the peace, enforce laws, serve process, execute judgments, and perform other such duties; the term is also sometimes used to refer to a deputy sheriff or sheriff's deputy.

shoplifting Stealing merchandise from a store.

solicitor The head legal officer of a city, town, department, or other body.

solitary confinement   Imprisoning someone alone in an isolated cell without contact with fellow prisoners or without any human contact at all, even from prison employees.

squatter   A person who sets up residence on property that does not belong to him or her.

stalk   To follow or watch a person in such a way that it alarms the person being followed and with no legitimate purpose. In many jurisdictions, stalking must involve multiple acts over a period of time with the intent of forcing the subject to form a relationship with the stalker.

stand   To appear in court when summoned to a trial.

stand mute   For a criminal defendant to refuse to plead when charged.

state law   Laws passed by and enforced within a state, as opposed to federal law.

statement   A written or verbal expression of some fact or belief; an assertion or allegation made by a witness.

state of mind   Mental condition at the time that some event occurs; a person's reasons for acting in a particular way.

state police   The police force hired by a state to keep the peace and enforce laws within a state.

statute   A formal written law passed by a legislature.

statutory   Related to statutes; required by or governed by a statute.

statutory rape   The crime of having sexual intercourse with a person below a statutorily prescribed age of consent, regardless of whether the victim consented and how old the victim claimed to be.

steal   To take something that belongs to someone else without the owner's consent intending to keep it or use it and never return it.

stealth   Cautious and secretive movement that is meant to go unnoticed.

subpoena   An official court document ordering a person to appear in court or at a judicial proceeding at a specified time.

summary judgment   A judgment that ends a lawsuit without trial in a case where a judge finds that there is no genuine issue of material fact and thus no need to send the matter to a jury.

summation   A last step in a jury trial before the jury begins deliberations, in which the attorneys for both sides sum up the evidence presented and call attention to the important points in their arguments; also called summing up.

summons A citation by an authority to appear before a court or judicial officer.

suspect A person who is believed to have committed a crime. Also used as a verb, meaning to believe without proof that someone has committed a crime or misdeed or to have some slight idea that something is the case without having any proof.

SWAT Special Weapons and Tactics unit; officers who specialize in getting violent situations under control.

take the Fifth To invoke the Fifth Amendment as justification for refusing to answer a question in a criminal prosecution.

tamper To interfere with something so as to change it, especially in a destructive or unauthorized way; to attempt to influence a jury through bribery or other illegal means.

tenant (1) A person who rents property from a landlord. (2) A person who owns or possesses property.

testify To speak under oath; to give evidence as a witness in a deposition or lawsuit; to serve as proof of something.

testimony The spoken evidence given by a witness under oath in court or at a deposition, or written evidence provided by a witness under oath through an affidavit.

theft The act of taking something that belongs to someone else without the owner's permission and with no intention of returning it; stealing.

third degree Thorough and prolonged questioning administered to a criminal suspect by the police with the intention of getting the person to confess to a crime.

third party A person who is not directly involved in a transaction; someone who is not a party to an agreement.

tort A private injury or wrong; a violation of a socially recognized duty owed to a plaintiff that results in injury to the plaintiff; torts can be caused intentionally, through negligence, or under strict liability.

trial A formal judicial proceeding in which a judge and sometimes a jury hear the evidence in a case and decide the rights of the parties in a civil case or the guilt or innocence of the defendant in a criminal case.

trial court The court in which a case is first presented, as opposed to an appellate court.

tribunal A judicial court; a judge's seat or bench; a judge or group of judges with jurisdiction in an area.

U.S. Marshal   An officer appointed by the president for a judicial district who executes all writs and orders issued by federal courts.

vagrant   A person with no regular job or home who wanders from place to place and supports himself or herself by begging.

vandalism   The act of willfully destroying or damaging property.

vehicular   Of or related to motor vehicles, such as automobiles and motorcycles.

verdict   A jury's or judge's finding on a question of fact, to be used by the court in determining its final judgment.

vice   Immorality; bad behavior; a bad habit; often used to describe crimes such as prostitution or drug use.

voyeur   A person who receives sexual gratification from watching other people engaged in sex acts or seeing other people naked, or from watching others in pain.

warrant   A written order issued by some authority directing someone to do a certain act, particularly an order issued by the state directing a law enforcement officer to arrest someone.

Chapter 6

Resources

The following resources—including organizations, books, periodicals, and Web sites—are valuable storehouses of information. Use them to gather industry facts as well as important contacts for further exploration.

Associations and Organizations

American Academy of Forensic Sciences (AAFS) is a 6,000-member organization of forensic professionals, including doctors, dentists, physical anthropologists, psychiatrists, engineers, lawyers, and other experts at examining dead bodies and ferreting the secrets out of crime scenes. The AAFS is committed to applying science to the law and educating the public about the forensic scientists. It publishes a journal, posts job listings, and sponsors an annual meeting. (http://www.aafs.org)

American Board of Forensic Anthropology (ABFA) is a nonprofit organization focusing on advancing the standards, practices, and scientific approaches of forensic anthropology. In addition, it offers certification programs and other educational opportunities for all levels of forensic anthropologists. (http://www.theabfa.org)

American Polygraph Association is an organization founded in 1966 and dedicated to upholding professional standards in polygraph testing. Their Web site is a good place to find schools that train students in lie detection and polygraph tests, a source of job listings, and a nice resource for information on the field. (http://www.polygraph.org)

International Association of Women Police (IAWP) is dedicated to the support of women in criminal justice careers. It publishes a magazine and holds annual conferences to discuss issues concerning women in law enforcement. Visit the Web site to learn about the history of women police, read job listings, and to research employment issues and learning opportunities. (http://www.iawp.org)

International Union of Police Associations (IUPA) is the main law enforcement union in the United States. Visit this Web site to learn about its history, its mission, legislative activities, membership, and more. (http://www.iupa.org)

National Latino Peace Officers Association (NLPOA) tries to help members with training in investigations, gangs, homeland security, immigration, and similar issues. The organization bears in mind that Latino and Hispanic law enforcement officers face challenges that are unique to their ethnicity. (http://www.nlpoa.org)

National Narcotic Officers' Associations' Coalition (NNOAC) traces its history to when police departments began fighting the drug epidemic in the 1960s, and gradually began developing specialized officers who were experts in drug enforcement. Over the years, many state law enforcement agencies formed narcotic officer associations to help organize drug enforcement operations and training. In 1994, those organizations came together in a national organization, the NNOAC, which works to represent narcotics officers at the national level. Visit the NNOAC Web site to find out about narcotics operations and to find links to narcotics officers' associations in different states. (http://www.natlnarc.org)

Books and Periodicals

Books

101 Reasons Why You Should Not Become A Cop. By James Richard Warner (iUniverse, 2005). Before investing too heavily in a criminal justice degree and the pursuit of a job in law enforcement, you should learn a little bit about the career. Law enforcement in real life is not the same as law enforcement on television. This book is full of honest interviews with real officers talking about their real lives, and there is no sugarcoating. The author does not necessarily want to discourage you from entering the field, but he does want you to know what you would be getting yourself into.

25 Biggest Mistakes Law Enforcement Officers Make and How to Avoid Them. By K. Karlberg (Tate Publishing and Enterprises, 2007). You do not want to make mistakes on the job, do you? It helps to know what those mistakes might be. Read this book to find out.

Becoming a Police Officer: An Insider's Guide to a Career in Law Enforcement. By Barry Baker (iUniverse, 2006). Detective Lieutenant Barry Baker worked for 32 years in the Baltimore Police Department, serving as a patrol officer, detective, sergeant, lieutenant, and special operations lieutenant. In his book, he describes the ups and downs of life in law enforcement in one of the more violent cities in the United States.

Criminal Investigation. By Karen M. Hess (Delmar Cengage Learning, 2009). This book, regularly updated, describes the essentials of conducting criminal investigations. The author covers forensics and physical evidence, photography, identity theft and cybercrime, preparing for court, terrorism, and many other topics.

Criminal Justice. By James Inciardi (McGraw-Hill, 2009). If you study criminal justice in college, you may find yourself using this textbook. Even if you do not, it might be worth flipping through the book in a library just to get a sense of what the field encompasses. It covers research methods, history, victims' perspectives on the criminal justice system, and includes profiles of famous criminals.

Dead Men Do Tell Tales: The Strange and Fascinating Cases of a Forensic Anthropologist. By William R. Maples and Michael Browning (Doubleday, 1994). Did you know that your skeleton is constantly changing? Growing, gaining weight, giving birth, and ageing all leave marks on your bones. So do weapons. Dr. Maples, a forensic anthropologist, explains how he uses this information to identify skeletons and in the process help law enforcement officials solve crimes. Part of his arsenal is a collection of tools and weapons that he uses to test wounds in bones to seek what caused the injuries. Forensic anthropology is not for the faint of heart or weak of stomach, but it certainly sounds interesting!

Emotional Survival for Law Enforcement: A Guide for Officers and Their Families. By Kevin M. Gilmartin (E-S Press, 2002). It is well known that law enforcement work is stressful for both

Best
Practice

Cross-Cultural Communications

All law enforcement officers should be aware of the variety of different cultures and ethnic groups living in the United States. *Multicultural Law Enforcement: Strategies for Peacekeeping in a Diverse Society*, by Robert M. Shusta et al (Upper Saddle River, NJ: Prentice Hall, 2010), now in its fifth edition, explores the way race, culture, and ethnicity affect communities and law enforcement. It covers gangs, immigrants, multi-racial groups, and the homeless, and offers strategies for officers hoping to build cross-cultural communications.

officers and their families. This book explores some of the reasons for that stress and offers some advice on how to deal with it.

Federal Law Enforcement Careers: Profiles of 250 High-Powered Positions and Tactics for Getting Hired. By Thomas Ackerman (JIST Works, 2006). Do your homework before starting your pursuit of a job in federal law enforcement. Really. If this is where your heart lies, you will be facing stiff competition and a very complicated hiring process. This book can help you position and sell yourself as a top candidate and navigate the intricacies of joining "the feds."

Great Jobs for Criminal Justice Majors. By Stephen Lambert (McGraw-Hill, 2007). So you have gone to college and earned a criminal justice degree. What to do now? Even if you started your program intending to become a law enforcement officer, you might consider some other possibilities. A criminal justice degree can lead to a job doing legal research, working as a victim's advocate, becoming a court administrator or bailiff, or any number of other choices that could keep you off the street.

J. Edgar Hoover: The Man and the Secrets. By Curt Gentry (W.W. Norton, 2001). If you are interested in learning about the development of the Federal Bureau of Investigation and the man who guided its growth for fifty years, this is a great book for you. Hoover ran the FBI from the mid-1920s through the mid-1970s, handling organized crime related to prohibition, World War II espionage, Cold War communist fears, and civil rights uprisings. In building up his organization, he amassed files on thousands of officially innocent people, recording their conversations in order to support accusations of disloyalty.

Law Enforcement Field Guide. By Eric Swanson (Informed Publishing, 2006). This book is waterproof and fits in a shirt pocket. That is great news, because you can carry it with you for quick information on how to handle arrests, criminal investigations, first aid, terrorism, going to court, and many other situations you may encounter in a day of law enforcement work.

Police Sergeant Examination Preparation Guide. By Larry F. Jetmore (Cliffs Notes, 2000). This book, written by a law enforcement officer, is intended to help readers improve their scores on the sergeant's examination. It contains a great deal of information on police supervision, an explanation of how multiple-choice written exams may be structured, practice questions, and test-taking techniques. It also explains the oral exams and provides advice on how to prepare for orals and handle situational exercises and assessment centers.

Police Technology. By Raymond E. Foster (Prentice Hall, 2004). Technology in law enforcement and criminal justice is constantly developing. This book is a good reference manual for the basics.

A Preparation Guide for the Assessment Center Method. By Tina Lewis Rowe (Charles C. Thomas, 2006). The assessment center test defeats many officers who attempt it. This book explains how these tests work and provides real-life examples of tests and situations. The book also contains a good deal of information on police supervision as well, making it useful for officers who simply want to improve their leadership skills.

Periodicals

American Police Beat aims to give a voice to the nation's law enforcement professionals. The magazine is dedicated to providing a forum where officers can exchange information and opinions about the many issues that impact their personal and professional lives on a monthly basis. (http://www.apbweb.com)

Law Enforcement Technology is a monthly magazine written for sworn officers who make most of the decisions for their units, including sergeants, captains, lieutenants, and other commanding officers. It reports on new technology and emerging trends and reviews companies and new products such as software, body armor, forensics technologies, and communications equipment. (http://www.officer.com/publication/pub.jsp?pubId=1)

Police: The Law Enforcement Magazine is ideal if you want to learn all about gangs, patrol, weapons, SWAT work, technology, and vehicles. It also has a Web site that posts job listings, archives of old articles, photo galleries, and has up-to-date forums and blogs. (http://www.policemag.com)

Web Sites

Bureau of Alcohol, Tobacco, Firearms and Explosives is the Web site for the ATF, a law enforcement agency within the Department of Justice that fights violent crime, trafficking in firearms, explosives, bombings, arson, terrorism, and illegal trafficking of alcohol and tobacco. Visit this Web site to learn about the agency's history, mission, activities, and career opportunities. (http://www.atf.gov)

California Highway Patrol is the largest state highway patrol/ state police agency in the country. Visit its Web site to read about its mission, its latest activities, and its job opportunities and training programs. (http://www.chp.ca.gov)

Department of Homeland Security maintains a Web site with information on the organization itself, its history, and its many activities. These include protecting border security, counterterrorism, preparedness, immigration, and many others. The department is almost always looking for employees; visit the Web site to find out about current opportunities. (http://www.dhs.gov)

DNA Initiative exists to ensure that forensic DNA technology advances criminal justice. This Web site contains articles about the use of forensic DNA, solving new and old crimes, information on efforts to reduce the backlog of DNA samples, links to state and federal statutes and case law related to DNA evidence, and many other resources. (http://www.dna.gov)

Federal Bureau of Investigation maintains a Web site, which describes the bureau's organization and its investigative priorities, gives advice on how to protect yourself from crime, and lists names of some of the most wanted fugitives from justice. (If you know where any of them are, contact the FBI!) You can also check up on breaking news to see how the fight against crime is going across the United States. (http://www.fbi.gov)

Everyone
Knows

Two Essential Sites

Law enforcement personnel have a large online presence. Visiting law enforcement Web sites is a great way to learn the ins and outs of the field and make contact with professional colleagues. PoliceOne.com and PoliceLink are both great places to read about daily concerns facing law enforcement officers and ways to deal with them.

PoliceOne (http://www.policeone.com) is full of news and information for law enforcement professionals. It posts breaking news from across the country, keeps up with trends in the field (Why do law enforcement officers not always wear seatbelts?), contains links to vendors of various law enforcement products, and has information on training and job opportunities. The Web site also posts regular videos of real law enforcement incidents along with lessons to be learned from them, such as in-car footage of actual pursuits and reminders about safe driving techniques.

Police Link (http://policelink.monster.com) has tons of the latest news and information for current law enforcement officers. You can find articles on law enforcement careers (many by foreword author Betsy Brantner Smith, police trainer and veteran of 29 years of police work in Chicago suburbs), recent news on police activities, reviews of gear, advice on becoming a cop, job listings, forums, and much more.

Federal Law Enforcement Training Center is operated by the Department of Homeland Security. It is the interagency law enforcement training organization for more than 80 federal agencies, and also assists local, state, and international law enforcement organizations. It is headquartered in Glynco, Georgia, and operates residential training sites in several other locations. Training programs include criminal investigator training programs for special agents, uniformed police training for uniformed officers, anti-terrorism intelligence awareness training for state and local agencies, and many more programs on basic and advanced topics. (http://www.fletc.gov)

Innocence Project works to identify people who have been wrongly convicted and prove that they are innocent of their crimes. This Web site has several articles on the reasons why people are incorrectly convicted, including eyewitness misidentification, improper forensic science, jailhouse snitches who lie on the stand, and false confessions. It also provides updates on various inmates thought to be innocent. (http://www.innocenceproject.org)

Law Enforcement and Tribal Courts are affiliated with the National Congress of American Indians, and track law enforcement issues facing American Indian tribes. This Web site contains a summary of major concerns and links to resources on matters of tribal justice. (http://www.ncai.org/Law-Enforcement-and-Tribal-Cou.34.0.html)

Los Angeles Police Department runs a Web site that is full of information for anyone interested in learning about police work. It contains a detailed history of the LAPD, a blog with first-hand accounts of daily police activities, new stories, crime maps, and much more. If you want to try a police career on for size, you can request to ride along in a police squad car one day; the LAPD receives more requests than it can accommodate, but you may be one of the lucky ones chosen. The Web site also contains information on hiring and training, and the department is almost always looking for good new officers. (http://www.lapdonline.org)

Los Angeles County Sheriff's Department is one of the largest in the nation. It is a good example of a county law enforcement Web site. It includes information on law enforcement operations, LASD services, news, achievements, crime maps, and job listings. Most counties have their own law enforcement Web sites. Google the name of your county and the word "sheriff" to find your local page. (http://www.lasd.org)

Office of Juvenile Justice and Delinquency Prevention has a department that concentrates on dealing with and preventing juvenile crime. Visit their Web site to get information on juvenile crime and the efforts the OJJDP is making to combat it. (http://ojjdp.ncjrs.gov)

Taser International is at the forefront of law enforcement technology, and is making more than just Taser shock-guns, such as their tactical, networkable computing and surveillance devices. The Web site also has useful information for physicians on how to remove Taser probes from the torso and extremities and for consumers on the legal status of the Taser. (http://www.taser.com)

Fast Facts

Origins of a Name

Everyone knows that police are often called "cops" for short. But where does that word come from? People have proposed various hypotheses about the origin of the word. One suggestion is that it is an abbreviation of "constable of police" or "constable on patrol," but that apparently is a myth. Others have proposed that "cop" is shortened from the word copper, referring to the copper badges worn by police officers. The consensus among historians seems to be that neither of these accounts is true, and that the word cop actually comes from the verb "cop," which means to take or seize. A police officer "cops" criminals when he arrests them, which makes him a "copper," or "cop" for short.

U.S. Drug Enforcement Administration is the federal agency entrusted with enforcing controlled substance laws. It fights organizations and groups that grow, manufacture, distribute, and otherwise traffic in controlled substances in the United States. The agency hires regularly, so visit their Web site to see if jobs are available. (http://www.justice.gov/dea)

U.S. Marshals Service maintains a Web site with facts and figures, investigative operations, judicial security, prisoner operations, tactical operations, witness security programs, alien transportation systems, and other programs pertaining to the service. There is also a section describing the history of the U.S. Marshals from the time George Washington appointed the first 13 marshals, a news section, and information about career opportunities with the organization. (http://www.justice.gov/marshals)

United States Secret Service has a Web site with information about this most exclusive career option. The student FAQs are especially useful. (http://www.secretservice.gov)

Index